D1426579

A Place in the Sun

Ultimate Escapes

A Place in the Sun

Ultimate Escapes

Fanny Blake

BOXTREE

First Published in 2004 by Boxtree,
an imprint of Pan Macmillan Ltd,
Pan Macmillan, 20 New Wharf Road, London N1 9RR, Basingstoke
and Oxford.
Associated companies throughout the world
www.panmacmillan.com

0 7522 1598 1

Introduction © Amanda Lamb 2004
Text © Fanny Blake 2004
Maps © Maps in Minutes™ 2004

A CIP catalogue record for this book is available from the British
Library.

Design by Perfect Bound Ltd
Colour reproduction by Aylesbury Studios Ltd
Printed and Bound in Great Britain by Bath Press

This book accompanies the television series *A Place in the Sun* made
by Freeform Productions for Channel 4.
Executive producers: Ann Lavelle and Antoine Palmer

Acknowledgements

Thanks go to Alasdair Riley and Melissa Loveday for their meticulous
help in researching this book.

Disclaimers

**The prices given for properties visited by house-hunters are
accurate for the exchange rate at the time of the visit.
Otherwise prices were accurate at the time of going to press.**

**The author, their assigns, licensees and printers cannot accept
liability for any errors or omissions contained herein nor
liability for any loss to any person acting as a result of the
information contained in this book. This book gives advice on
the basis that readers contemplating buying a property abroad
take their own professional advice.**

Picture credits

Jamie Fry: 7
Australian Tourist Commission: 5 (top picture), 8/9, 12, 13, 15, 16,
18, 19, 20, 23, 27, 28, 43
Tourism Queensland: 24, 32/33, 34
Tourism New South Wales: 31, 37
Visit Florida: 5 (second picture down), 44/45, 50, 60, 61, 68
Maine Office of Tourism: 48, 49, 62
Virginia Tourism Corporation: 51, 71
www.picturescolourlibrary.co.uk: 52 (© Monica Wells), 74 (© David
Noble), 85 (© Colin Paterson)
Travel Ink: 53 (© Cristian Barnett), 155 (© Abbie Enock)
Mississippi Development Authority / Division of Tourism: 54
Sylvia Cordaiy Photo Library Ltd: 55 (© Ian Leonard), 67 (© Dorothy
Burrows), 70 (© Humphrey Evans), 131 (© Paul Jeffrey), 136, 139
(© Johnathan Smith)
Arizona Office of Tourism: 56, 58
Robert Holmes / California Tourism: 57, 59, 65, 66
The Travel Library: 63, 141
Greater Boston Convention and Visitors' Bureau: 64, 69
Rhode Island Tourism Division: 72
South African Tourism: 5 (third picture down), 87/88, 90, 92, 95, 96,
98, 101, 102, 104, 107, 108, 111, 112, 119
Bahamas Tourist Office: 2, 5 (bottom picture), 120/121, 145
Eye Ubiquitous: 124, 128, 130, 133, 135
Tradewind Realty Ltd: 127
Caribbean Way: 142
All other pictures © Freeform Productions

Contents

Introduction

By Amanda Lamb

Welcome to *A Place in the Sun: Ultimate Escapes*. It's a great read with fabulous pictures, great advice and useful information about the countries we have visited with a whole host of new househunters hoping to find their own piece of paradise.

I can't believe it has been four years since I started filming *A Place in the Sun*, and I am still loving every minute of it. We have travelled all over the world, and helped all sorts of people, with different budgets and different needs to find their own ideal place in the sun. From a chic city apartment, to a tumble-down cottage, miles from its nearest neighbour, we have put the househunters in touch with local experts and helped them to consider the pros and cons of each property they've looked at, so they can make an informed decision – even if that sometimes means they need to keep looking!

We have also started to find that, as well as the househunters who want something a short hop away in Europe, there are increasingly Britons who are looking for paradise further afield. In this book we are going to look at the far-flung destinations and the long-haul locations that are attracting the most attention from househunters searching for their dream home: Australia, the USA, South Africa and the Caribbean. The world has become a much smaller place and the influences of television from America and Australia mean that these countries feel much closer to home. Of course we are also united by a common language, which makes not only the buying of property more straight forward, but also makes it easier to order dinner in a restaurant. And with the long hours of sunshine, the big blue skies and the amazing landscapes, there is more than enough incentive to buy in these beautiful countries. Long sandy beaches, dramatic mountains, buzzing cities, lush vineyards and vast open prairies – who could ask for more?

Just one word of caution before you take the plunge and sell up to move to the sun: this book is intended as an introduction and a general guide to buying property abroad and living in the countries featured. If you are serious about buying a property abroad you should seek professional advice, and any costs incurred employing a solicitor or financial advisor could save you from making a very expensive mistake. Remember though, owning a property abroad can be a very rewarding experience, not to mention a worthwhile investment under the right circumstances. There are some fantastic properties out there just waiting to be discovered, so happy house hunting!

Amanda Lamb, 2004

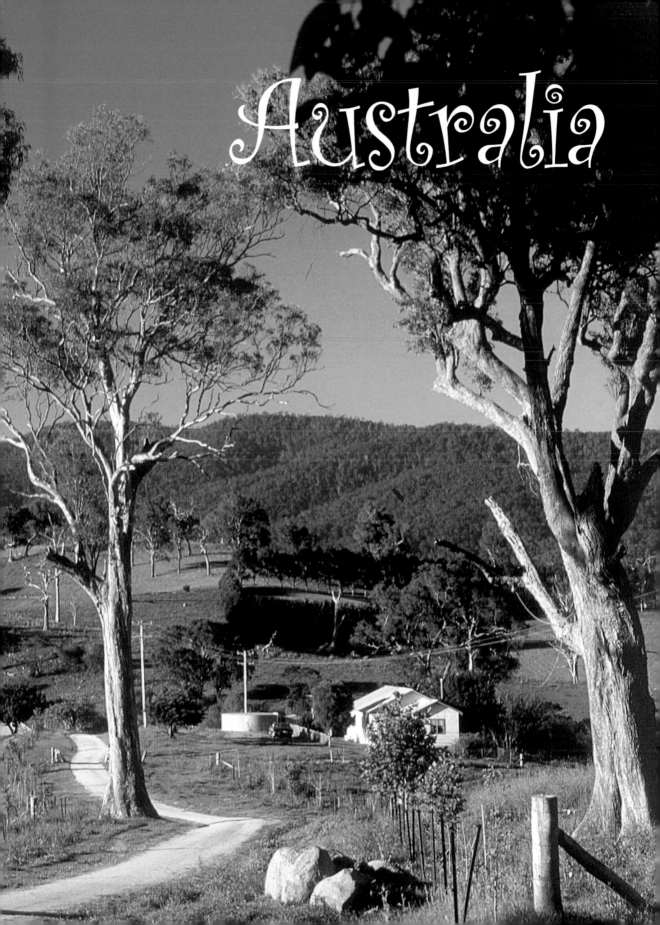

Australia

Introduction

Australia is simply unique. Its promises of sunshine, freedom and prosperity have attracted foreign residents for years. It is the largest island (roughly thirty times the size of the UK), the smallest continent and the sixth largest country in the world. The lure of a life in the great outdoors attracts people from all over the world looking for new opportunities and a new start.

Divided into the six states of Western Australia, South Australia, Queensland, New South Wales, Victoria and Tasmania, and two territories, Northern Territory and Australian Capital Territory, Australia offers a wide diversity of landscapes. The interior is largely made up of vast red deserts, or the Outback, interrupted by mountain ranges, weird rock formations and salt lakes with the scrubby 'bush' lying between it and a coastline strung with modern cosmopolitan cities and resorts. The mountainous Great Dividing Range runs parallel to and protects the length of the eastern seaboard where by far the majority of the population live. There the coastline is washed by Pacific Ocean with the Great Barrier Reef, the largest reef in the world, running parallel with the Great Dividing Range from Cape York in the north of Queensland as far south as Fraser Island.

The climate is as variable as the landscape. The tropical north gives way to more temperate weather further south with winter snow falling in the mountain ranges of New South Wales and Victoria. Of course to us Brits the seasons are reversed so that Christmas Day can be spent on a baking hot beach while the ski season in the Snowy Mountains (NSW and Victoria) kicks off in June. There are more square kilometres of ski slopes in Australia than in Europe.

Australia boasts fifteen UNESCO World Heritage Sites, among them the Great Barrier Reef; Kakadu National Park in the north; Willandra Lakes Region where archaeological finds date back 40,000 years; the Tasmanian Wilderness; the Lord Howe Island Group off New South Wales; Central Eastern Rainforest Reserves (Australia); Uluru-Kata Tjuta National Park; Wet Tropics of Queensland; Shark Bay, Western Australia; Fraser Island; Australian Fossil Mammal Sites (Riversleigh/Naracoorte); Heard and McDonald Islands; Macquarie Island; Greater Blue Mountains Area; Purnululu National Park.

Sport is one of the main leisure activities, ranging from Australian rules football to cricket, surfing and all manner of water-based activities and extreme sports. In recent years, they have become as well known for their restaurant and café society as the ubiquitous beer and barbies. Public services are good with high standards in health care and education plus excellent communication systems. But alongside all the modernity exists one of the world's oldest cultures. Australian Aboriginals have lived in the country for at least 60,000 years. Over the years since discovery by the West, they have been dispossessed and discriminated against, yet their culture is still evident. Today, moves have been made to include them in the multi-culturalism that characterizes Australia.

Previous page: Bega Valley Shire in coastal New South Wales, runs from Bermagui to the Victorian border. It boasts unspoilt beaches, coastal lakes, National Parks and quiet urban areas.

facts

Capital: Canberra

Area: 7,686,850 sq km

Highest point: Mount Kosciusko (2,229 m)

Lowest point: Lake Eyre (-15 m)

Coastline: 25,760 km

Population: 19,731,984

Currency: Australian dollar (AUD)

Time zone: GMT + 12 hours (Sydney)

Electricity: 240V at 50Hz

Weights and measures: Metric

Religions: Anglican, Catholic

Language: English

Government: Democratic, federal state system that recognizes the British monarch as sovereign

International dialling code: 00 61

National holiday: 26 January, Australia Day

Once a sleepy coastal hideaway, Byron Bay has become one of New South Wales' most popular resorts with a lively arts and social scene.

This is a country of grand extremes, of space, sunshine and the good life. For anyone looking for a new life down under, they will find all they could wish for in spades.

new south wales – the first state

New South Wales is where it all began. In 1788 the first fleet of British convict ships docked in Botany Bay, eight years after its discovery by Captain James Cook. Unexpectedly inclement weather and the appearance of a couple of French ships drove the fleet north to Port Jackson, now part of Sydney Bay. Those early settlers endured appalling conditions to be eventually relieved by the arrival of more supplies, convicts (until 1840), and free settlers. Over the years, the colony developed and expanded, eventually becoming the dynamic sun-kissed city of **Sydney** that we know today. Known for its Opera House (1973) and Harbour Bridge, Sydney also offers a good slice of colonial history in areas such as The Rocks.

New South Wales is the most heavily populated state of Australia with most of its residents concentrated along the one thousand plus kilometres of Pacific coastline. Renowned for its first-rate stretches of sandy beaches, its bays and inlets, this is the place for surf-seekers, sun lovers and water-sport enthusiasts. The climate in the north is semi-tropical becoming more temperate towards the south. The coastline north of Sydney is strung with popular holiday resorts. Among them **Nelson Bay** perched on the tip of Port Stephens Bay close to the quieter towns of **Hawks Nest** and **Tea Garden**; **Port Macquarie**, koala capital of Australia, once a penal colony now flanked by residential suburbs; **Coffs Harbour** has seen considerable residential development while maintaining its natural beauty; **Byron Bay**, the laid-back surfers' paradise. Between the rain forest and the sea lies Lismore, centre of **Rainbow Region**, an area known for its weekend markets, macadamia nut plantations, rainforests, nature reserves, waterfalls and historic villages. South of Sydney the coastline is more relaxed, less tourist-driven though with no shortage of resorts and picturesque fishing villages.

Inland, the Great Dividing Range splits the state in two. Few intrepid souls live west of it. However there are possibilities of a rewarding rural life in areas of outstanding natural beauty, not too far from the bustle of the coast. In the north, the **New England** plateau provides good arable and pasture land. Among the main towns are: **Armidale**, surrounded by superb mountain scenery and known as a university city; **Glen Innes**, located high in the gem mining area; **Gunnedah**, a centre for wheat and stock sales; **Tamworth**, country music capital of Australia; **Tenterfield**, the charming historic birthplace of the Australian Federation. A little to the south, a landscape of vineyards stretches across the **Hunter Valley**, home to some of the greatest wine producers in the world. Surrounding all this are numerous breathtaking national parks and nature reserves. Venturing into the southern highlands south-west of Sydney, old colonial mansions and homesteads enjoy the cooler climate to this day.

South-west of Sydney, tranquillity is guaranteed in the **Blue Mountains**, named after the effect of the eucalyptus oil which causes a blue haze. Here picturesque small towns and villages, many of them linked by the great Western Highway, enjoy

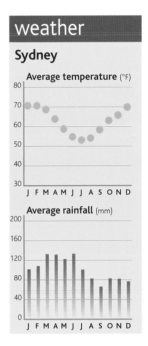

weather

Sydney

Average temperature (°F)

80
70
60
50
40
30

J F M A M J J A S O N D

Average rainfall (mm)

200
160
120
80
40
0

J F M A M J J A S O N D

For a taste of gold rush days, the New South Wales town of Adelong and its surrounding countryside has plenty of reminders.

spectacular vantage points. Each one of them has its own history, sights and culture. Highlights among them are **Leura** where any residential developments fall into the strict guidelines of the town with heritage colours; **Katoomba**, the largest town with spectacular views. Due south of Sydney are the **Snowy Mountains**, where Australia's highest mountain, **Mount Kosciusko**, rears its head. From June to October, the ski season dominates the region, while in the summer, the towns make great bases for spectacular walking.

The **western region** of NSW boasts a number of well-preserved historic towns built with money from the Gold Rush. Some towns have barely survived since those days and local wealth is now derived from the fertile agricultural plains which are good for the vineyards surrounding **Mudgee**, apple and cherry orchards. **Bathurst** boasts some splendid Victorian architecture alongside a thriving café culture; **Orange** is a pleasant town with plenty of cafés and restaurants; **Dubbo**, strong in colonial history and architecture, is famed for its zoo as well as being the gateway to the outback. **Wagga Wagga**, the other principal frontier town, is known for its wines and plethora of gardens.

Canberra, the political and administrative capital of Australia, is its only major inland city. It was planned in 1908 by the American architect Walter Burley Griffin after the decision was taken to establish a new city to end any competition between Melbourne and Sydney. Situated in a valley in the southern tableland of NSW, it has plenty of open spaces, parkland and attractive leafy suburbs. All the major buildings are built around Lake Burley Griffin in the Parliamentary Triangle. To the south of the city lies the rugged Namadgi National Park – aboriginal paintings at Yankee Hat Rock.

Visit www.visitnsw.com.au for tourist information.

queensland – the sunshine state

Queensland, famously home to the Great Barrier Reef, is also known as the Sunshine State and is Australia's ultimate outdoor playground with almost 7,500 kilometres of coastline. The second largest state in Australia, its capital city is **Brisbane** where modern glass buildings rub shoulders with sandstone heritage buildings and traditional wooden houses with new suburbs springing up on the periphery. The Brisbane River loops round the city centre where a central shopping mall, imposing historic buildings, plenty of alfresco cafés and weekend markets contribute to a relaxed cosmopolitan atmosphere. The subtropical climate promises warm days and balmy nights and is so loved by retirees that it's nicknamed 'Bris-Vegas'.

South of Brisbane lies the **Gold Coast**, Australia's answer to the Costa del Sol, with 70 kilometres of surf beaches renowned the world over which are overlooked by a busy sprawl of high-rise living, bars and clubs centred on Surfer's Paradise. If you're looking for something more peaceful, head south towards Coolangatta or inland towards the Lamington and Springbrook national parks where untouched subtropical rainforest enjoys cooler temperatures and unforgettable scenery.

North of Brisbane is the **Sunshine Coast**. Less frenetic than its neighbour, it divides neatly into three regions centred on the seaside town of **Caloundra** in the

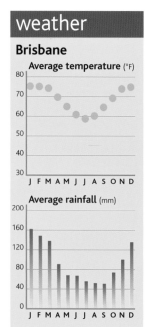

weather

Brisbane

Average temperature (°F)

Average rainfall (mm)

south; **Maroochy** in the centre with its resorts of **Maroochydore**, **Alexandra Heads** and **Mooloolaba**; **Noosa Heads** in the north, a much loved celebrity haunt and site of some of the most desirable real estate in Australia. Off the coast lies **Fraser Island**, the largest sand island in the world and a UNESCO world heritage site. The spectacular Glasshouse Mountains mark the start of the hinterland. Dotted with delightful villages that attract artists and craftsmen, the landscape of dairy pastures, pineapple plantations and sugarcane is interrupted by pockets of rain forest. The principal communities are **Maleny**, **Montville** and **Mapleton** where traditional log and stone homes blend with more modern architecture.

Surfers' Paradise on Queensland's Gold Coast has a perfect beach that makes it an ideal spot for families.

The **central Queensland Coast** between Rockhampton and Cairns offers more beaches, more quiet coastal towns, more rural hinterland and more heat. The tropic of Capricorn is marked in **Rockhampton**, the beef capital of Australia, a bright, friendly city sitting astride the Fitzroy River with many listed historic buildings. The tropics start further north, past Townsville, where the coastal mountain ranges dip to the sea wreathed in cloud and lush vegetation. **Townsville** itself is a vibrant town boasting the best inner city beachfront in Australia that's lined with cafés, bars and recreational facilities. **Cairns** is the second biggest tourist destination in Australia after Sydney thanks to its proximity to the Great Barrier Reef, Atherton Tableland, one of the richest farming areas in Queensland, and the Wet Tropics Rainforest.

Queensland is rich in natural resources, its principal products being wool, grain, meat and sugar. It also offers a fantastic outdoor lifestyle. It has a reputation as the most conservative state perhaps because of the number of retirees who head there.

Visit www.destinationqueensland.com for tourist information.

victoria – the garden state

Victoria is the smallest Australian state but it offers just as much as the others in the way of relaxation, entertainment, colonial history or full-on adventure. Coming this far south, you'll find a climate more European and a population as familiar with rain as the English. The state offers a wealth of different landscapes from the wild Grampian mountain ranges to the Yarra vineyards, from the rainforest of Gippsland to the Victoria Alps, from the fertile plains of the Murray river to the white-sanded beaches of the Bellarine Peninsula.

Its capital **Melbourne** offers a wide range of attractions. The city prospered in the mid-nineteenth century at the time of the Gold Rush and was the country's capital until 1927 when Canberra took over the role. Widely perceived as Australia's cultural centre, it is now home to much of the country's film and TV industry, the Australian Ballet Company, many museums and galleries, and hosts a number of prestigious annual sporting events. Melbourne is plum in the middle of the state's rugged coastline where beach culture thrives. Its suburbs encroach onto the Mornington Peninsula where the beaches are crowded. North of the Dandenong Ranges lies the Yarra Valley, both scenic and home to some of the great wine producers.

To the east of the city lies the **Gippsland** region where the fertile land is used for dairy farming. Highlights here are Wilson's Promontory National Park, a spit of protected land that once joined to Tasmania, and the Gippsland lakes separated

With its nineteenth century architecture, theatres, bookshops, galleries and notoriously wet weather, Melbourne is considered the most European of Australian cities.

from the ocean by Ninety Mile Beach. Behind the sandy beaches are picturesque rural towns, thick forestland and mountainous terrain. In the north-east lie the ski resorts, principal among them **Mount Buller**, **Falls Creek** and **Mount Hotham**, popular in the summer as bases for fishing and trekking.

To the west of Melbourne, the **Great Ocean Road** is the principal link between the laid-back coastal towns and fishing villages, as it runs east to west from **Geelong** to **Warrnambool** cutting through the densely forested mountainous coastline. The road was built after the First World War employing ex-service men and those put out of work during the Depression. All surfies head to **Torquay**, focus of the surfing community. **Lorne** is a popular retreat for those seeking a break from the capital and hosts the largest blue water swimming competition in the world. One of the most popular stretches of road runs through the Port Campbell National Park. Historic towns include **Queenscliff** with its picturesque fishermen's cottages and impressive Victorian architecture, **Port Campbell** and **Port Fairy**, both with numerous listed residential buildings. Only a shortish drive north-west of Melbourne lie the **Goldfields** where the two main cities of **Ballarat** and **Bendigo** are particularly good examples of the architectural heritage from the Gold Rush with their wide streets, ornate houses and large public gardens. In the north-west, the Murray River winds its way down to the sea through prosperous farmlands, old homesteads and river port towns such as **Wentworth** with its many gracious buildings including the country's first gaol; **Mildura**, surrounded by wineries, citrus orchards and national parks, **Swan Hill** and **Echuca** with its nostalgic feel for bygone days.

Visit www.tourismvictoria.com for tourist information.

south australia – the festival state

Eighty per cent of the state of South Australia is outback yet over 99.25 per cent of the population is packed into the remaining 20 per cent. Major attractions include the Barossa valley, home of wines of international repute, a stunning coastline particularly around the Eyre and Yorke peninsulas and towns that range from the sophisticated capital of Adelaide to the remote opal-mining town of Coober Pedy. The history of South Australia is quite distinct from that of the other states on the eastern seaboard. It had been home to Australia's largest population of Aboriginals for 10,000 years until an English entrepreneur, Edward Wakefield, meticulously planned the development of the state. This was to be a country of free settlers, not convicts, the first of whom arrived in 1836. By the 1840s, the discovery of copper brought an influx of Cornish miners and good fortune for the inhabitants. In 1894, South Australia became the second country in the world (after New Zealand) to grant the vote to women. Yet, until the 1970s, South Australia was known for its conservatism, both social and political. Change came with the appointment of Don Dunstan, the Labour premier who liberalized the state, introducing Aboriginal land-rights legislation, outlawing racialism, decriminalizing homosexuality and abolishing capital punishment.

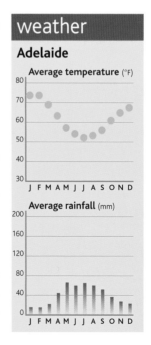

weather

Adelaide

Average temperature (°F)

Average rainfall (mm)

Adelaide was designed by William Light, the Surveyor General, so that its neat grid pattern incorporates attractive public squares and gardens. The city spans the Torrens River and is surrounded by parkland. Between the imposing tree-lined North Terrace and the river lies the town's cultural centre where a number of impressive nineteenth-century buildings may be found, including the state library, art gallery and museum and two university campuses. There is a thriving café culture, especially around Rundle Street, with plenty of restaurants, bars, a buzzing nightlife and a busy arts scene. The city boasts two festivals: the biennial Adelaide Festival, fortifying Adelaide's claim to be the artistic capital of Australia, and the annual Womadelaide Music Festival held in the Botanic Park. In the lively suburb of Northern Adelaide lie elegant colonial mansions and attractive bluestone cottages. Other suburbs are spread a long way from the city centre, all with their own local character affording plenty of space, greenery and a relaxed atmosphere.

Head out of Adelaide and within forty minutes, you'll be hiking in the sublime Adelaide Hills or savouring the delights of the **MacLaren Vale** wineries tucked into the **Fleurieu Peninsular** between the Mount Lofty Ranges and the Gulf St Vincent. Just off the peninsular lies Kangaroo Island with a wealth of good beaches, native animal life and unusual rock formations. The south-east coastline has great beaches that offer excellent surfing as well as quieter fishing, canoeing and swimming opportunities along the coastal Coorong National Park. There's little concentrated tourist development here, just several attractive fishing ports such as **Victor Harbor**, **Port Elliot**, **Robe**, **Beachport** and **Millicent**.

North of Adelaide lies the **Barossa Valley** originally colonized by Germans fleeing persecution. It offers a peaceful rural landscape, dotted with small villages, wineries of international renown and sheep farms. **Lyndoch** is the oldest town while close by the originally German settlements of **Bethany** and **Tanunda** boast historic dwellings and a quiet country atmosphere. **Ariootpa** is the Valley's commercial centre and home to Penfold's winery while to its south-east lies **Angaston**, a pretty town with two parks, a creek at its centre and examples of colonial architecture. There are excellent opportunities for cyclists and walkers throughout the region but perhaps its main attraction lies in its excellent restaurants and of course the wineries.

The Barossa Valley is one of Australia's best wine regions. Its undulating countryside is dotted with small villages, stone cottages and grand wine estates.

To the west of Adelaide lie the **Yorke and Eyre Peninsulas**, both major wheat and barley producing regions. The 'copper triangle' of the Yorke Peninsula was originally colonized by Cornish miners whose heritage is still seen in the church and cottage architecture, familiar names and even the Cornish pasty. The Eyre Peninsula is known for its 2,000 kilometres of rugged coastline splintered with shipwrecks. **Port Lincoln** is situated on Boston Bay, one of the world's largest natural harbours. It is the busiest of the resort towns in a region popular for its whale-watching, surfing and fishing. The area around **Coffin Bay** located on a particularly beautiful estuary is popular for all watersports.

Other highlights of the state include: the Flinders Ranges with its spectacular natural basin of Wilpena Pound; the Murray River, flanked by orchards, pastures and vineyards, a haven for all boating enthusiasts; the vast wilderness of the Nullarbor Plain.

Visit www.southaustralia.com for tourist information.

Rich farmland gives way to forested hills in the majestic shadow of the Flinders Ranges in South Australia.

western australia — the wildflower state

By far the largest state, Western Australia occupies about one third of the Australian continent and is at least ten times the size of the UK. Occupied by aboriginals for thousands of years, Western Australia was brought to the attention of the West by a Dutchman, Dirk Hartog in 1616. It was two hundred years later that the British got round to colonizing it. Most of it is arid desert land so the population (currently standing at almost two million) has gravitated to the coast and the conducive climate of its capital city Perth that faces out to the Indian Ocean. Ten per cent of all Australians live in WA and three-quarters of them live in **Perth**, considered to be the most isolated city in the world. It was Captain James Stirling who founded the Swan River Colony, later Perth, in 1829. From 1850 to 1868, convicts were used as labour in the construction of buildings and the city's infrastructure. In the 1880s the Gold Rush brought prosperity to the area and at the beginning of the twentieth century a telegraph cable finally connected Perth with South Africa and London, and a railway was built that ran from Kalgoorlie across to the eastern states.

Today the city's residents enjoy an enviable lifestyle in a streamlined modern city on the banks of the Swan, with fabulous white-sanded beaches and a wonderful climate. Perth is a relatively small city, with a few historic buildings holding their own among the omnipresent steel and glass high rises. To the west, the residential suburbs of **Cottesloe**, **Claremont**, **Nedlands** and **Subiaco** are among those conveniently close to the beach. Take the train, following the direction of the Swan, and you'll come to the charming port of **Fremantle**, once a penal settlement now a city in its own right, with a laid-back atmosphere, Victorian buildings and popular

Built on the banks of the Swan River, Perth's appeal lies in its green spaces and its proximity to the ocean.

'cappuccino strip'. Heading inland, there is little to attract the ex-pat homebuyer, unless tempted by the attractions of the Swan or Avon Valleys. The Swan valley supports various wineries while the Avon Valley boasts some of the oldest towns of Western Australia, in particular **York**, an appealing town with plenty of well-preserved Victorian architecture.

Thanks to its reliably sunny climate, south-west of Perth has attracted much development. **Margaret River** produces international class wines but is also known for its great surfing beaches and the towering karri forests. The climate is cooler and the ocean wilder. Sleepy country towns bask in the sunshine, good restaurants are often attached to wineries, and optimistic surfers await the perfect wave. By the coast, the modest towns such as **Bunbury** and **Busselton** lead the way. Life down here is quiet, relaxed and appealing. The main city on the Rainbow Coast is **Albany**, first founded in 1826 and Western Australia's principal port until the building of Fremantle. Moderate temperatures, stunning scenery and local history all make it an attractive place for many Perth weekenders. North of the most northern suburbs of Perth tends not to attract the foreign homebuyer although there are plenty of tourist attractions. The climate changes from the Mediterranean temperature of Perth to tropical in the far north. However that's no reason not to journey into the hotter north on the road to the pearl-fishing centre of **Broome**, passing through small resort towns, fabulous beaches and chances to experience the geological wonders of the Pinnacles Desert and the Bungle Bungles.

Visit www.westernaustralia.com for tourist information.

northern territory – outback australia

Aboriginals have lived in the Northern Territory for thousands of years. Today they make up one in five of the total population of under two million. The British handed the control of the state over to the colony of South Australia in 1863. Six years later General Goyder led an expedition that succeeded in establishing a settlement at what is now known as Darwin. In 1872 the arrival of the Overland Telegraph Line from South Australia served to link Australia with the rest of the world.

The two main centres in the Northern Territory are **Darwin** and **Alice Springs**. Sweltering in permanent temperatures around 30 °C, Darwin has no alternative but to adopt a chilled-out lifestyle. Destroyed once by the Japanese during the Second World War and again by Cyclone Tracy in 1974, today's city is a modern one, offering all the benefits and the life found in any other Australian state capital. Streets lined with palms, bamboo and mango palms and brilliant flowering tropical shrubs, fabulous beaches, outdoor living, a multitude of sporting activities, and one of Australia's finest harbours, are some of the attractions on offer. However, few British homebuyers venture this far north unless they are simply exploring the highlights of the region, among which are the monolithic and mystical Uluru in the red centre, the Kakadu National Park and the spectacular Katherine Gorge.

Visit www.northernterritory.com for tourist information.

websites

www.domain.com.au – the website of the property section of the *Sydney Morning Herald*

www.reiaustralia.com.au – website of the Real Estate Institute of Australia with links to all states

www.immi.gov.au – Australian government's official website for the Department of Immigration and Multicultural and Indigenous Affairs

www.australia.org.uk – website of the UK Australian High commission

The property market

Australia has been a magnet for migrants, especially British, for 200 years. Although the days of the £10 assisted boat passage for '£10 Poms' have long since gone, this vast country has evolved into a top-of-the-list destination for those wishing to up sticks and make a new home in the 'lucky country'. One in ten foreigners buying into Australia today is from Britain.

The difference yesterday and today is that Australia can now afford to be picky about its immigrants and chooses those who will make a contribution. There is an unofficial expectation that those who decide to set up home in Australia will demonstrate their commitment by buying a property. It's an Oz thing. Home ownership down under runs at about 70 per cent of the population, which is one of the highest rates in the world. There is also a healthy rental market, which is a bonus for those who wish to dip their toe in the property waters before taking the plunge and buying.

Being get-up-and-go and so huge, Australia has embraced new technology as the perfect communications tool, especially among estate agents showcasing their properties which are as varied as their homeland is big. Anyone seriously considering buying a home down under should include the Internet in their research. They will soon discover that Australian estate agents seem to compete with each other to design bigger and better websites.

First cyber visits should be to the Real Estate Institute for each of the six states. Although these professional bodies exist mainly for the benefit of their members, their websites are packed with information for the consumer, including those in search of residential properties. This goldmine ranges from archives of newspaper articles and press releases to easy-to-understand statistics on property prices and trends. There are also invaluable links to websites for member estate agents in specific areas.

The Australian property market boomed in the late 1990s, and has risen steadily since then, despite occasional scare stories that the bubble would burst. Even so, most residential property sells for less than £200,000, and as recently as late 2003 the average price of a residential home across the country was £120,000.

And bear in mind that the unbroken rule of property markets worldwide – that location is the number one pricing factor – is particularly marked in Australia. A house in one of the country's two most expensive cities, Sydney and Melbourne, can cost almost twice as much as its equivalent in Adelaide or Perth, and so on across the property landscape. East coast city prices, especially for luxury apartments with water views to die for, shadow their London equivalent. But, in the main, it is reasonable to expect to be able to trade up from a SE England semi to an Australian home with patio, barbie, pool and other extras you would not get in the UK.

Well-to-do residents of the four major eastern cities, looking for a weekend home beside the sea, are now prepared to drive further and further afield, perhaps two hours and more, to find a substantial family property for around £400,000.

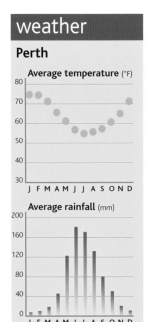

weather

Perth

Average temperature (°F)

80
70
60
50
40
30

J F M A M J J A S O N D

Average rainfall (mm)

200
160
120
80
40
0

J F M A M J J A S O N D

Although an Australian national newspaper said recently: 'If you are looking for that elusive seaside shack, and all you've got is a million dollars … dream on', it is still possible to find such properties in seaside towns and cities north of Perth.

Still, with careful planning and research, it is quite possible to make that Australian dream come true for far less.

The Sydney market is overblown and prices can be outrageous. There has been talk of a property downturn for about three years, but there is still no real sign of it.

types of property

Perhaps you want to buy into the traditional Aussie dream of a home set in a quarter of an acre in the suburbs. Why not? Of course, an Australian suburb bears no comparison to its UK counterpart. In 'the lucky country' a typical suburban home conjures up not only space and privacy, two or three bedrooms, parking for two cars and little extras such as laundry room and balconies, but also guaranteed barbie, perhaps a swimming pool, and more likely or not public tennis courts and other sports facilities just around the corner.

The prospective homeowner, seeking something a little more adventurous than the ubiquitous cookie-cutter house in the suburbs, is faced with a bewildering choice in each state, let alone the whole country. It ranges from striking high-rise apartments in concrete, steel and glass to wooden houses raised on stilts.

Taken at random: a Melbourne estate agent advertises various properties across a spectrum which includes 'Art Deco, Spanish Missions, Queen Anne,

Victorian, Colonial, Edwardian and Federation'. Confused? You will be when you listen to the expert in Canberra who identifies a dozen styles of local twentieth-century architecture, from inter-war functionalism to late twentieth-century stripped classical. Sometimes you find half-a-dozen contrasting styles side by side in one street.

Historical heritage commands respect, adding a premium to old properties. You would expect to pay much more for a 200-year-old Federation Period red-brick single-storey cottage, with stained-glass windows and a roof extending over a large veranda, than you would for a neighbouring brick bungalow of the same size, built in the mid-twentieth century.

So much for period houses. The Australian government's policy is to channel foreign investment into the home property market in the form of new housing. As explained elsewhere, any property transaction undertaken by buyers not holding either an Australian passport or permanent visa, must be Government-approved. And it is relatively easier to get official approval if the intention is to buy new or off-plan housing. Because no more than 50 per cent of new developments can be sold to foreign buyers, it makes sense to purchase at the first point of release – after all, you get first dibs at the best view.

An idea of the scale of the vast off-plan and new-build market can be got by looking at properties coming onstream all the time from one company alone –

Mirvac, one of the country's leading property groups for the past three decades. Their website (www.mirvac.com.au) features thousands of houses and apartments in or near all major cities and dozens of towns. They range from off-the-peg house designs to cutting-edge high-rise modernity, including retirement homes in niche developments catering to over-fifty-fives.

Whatever headache you get doing your sums – in particular, keeping up with rising prices – the pain is alleviated by the knowledge that your budget continues to stretch much further in Australia than in the UK. Pound for dollar, the terraced house in a British city suburb translates into an Aussie dream home.

But, to state the obvious, your budget buys much more in some parts of Australia. Its cities and their suburbs are booming, but some are twice as expensive as others. You only have to look at the statistics, not only state-wide, but local.

For example, in late 2003 when the exchange rate was about £1 = $2.45A, the median price of an established house in Sydney, Australia's most expensive city and capital in all but name, was £190,000. This compared with Melbourne (£150,000), Canberra (£125,000), Brisbane (£120,000), Adelaide (£90,000), Perth (£86,000), Darwin (£84,000) and Hobart (£75,000). In some cases, these were rises of about 50 per cent over three years – and sometimes more, so assume these prices have risen since these statistics were compiled.

Sydneysiders are obsessed with property ('How much did you pay for this place?' is one of the first questions they want to ask, and often do) and are prepared to pay over the odds for anything with water views, be it river, harbour or sea. Those who want the buzz of upmarket waterside city living, but cannot afford Sydney, might consider New Quay Melbourne's new docklands development (the equivalent of Sydney's Circular Quay) where 22,000 apartments are due to be completed in 2005.

The country's third largest city Brisbane, with its distinctive sandstone architecture, is emerging from the shadows of Sydney and Melbourne, thanks to a programme of urban regeneration and property development. Not so long ago a small country town, it is now a cosmopolitan melting pot, attracting prospective homeowners with a vast choice of high-rise riverfront apartments, desirable suburb houses and beachfront properties.

Of course, Australia is far from being all city life. It is often the great outdoors, the beach and the country, which attracts British buyers. Recent popular choices for Britons, apart from obvious destinations such as the touristy Gold Coast south of Brisbane, include Tasmania, the unspoilt heart-shaped island, about the size of Scotland, 200 miles off the southernmost tip of Australia, where the weather is much like back home in the UK.

The Noosa region, on Queenland's Sunshine Coast north of Brisbane, is proving popular. So too is the coast around Geelong in Victoria, where increasing numbers of Melbourne city-dwellers, 125 miles away, have second homes. Just look at the statistics, though, and you will see that real estate in the west of Australia is much cheaper than anything to be found to the east, especially on the coast.

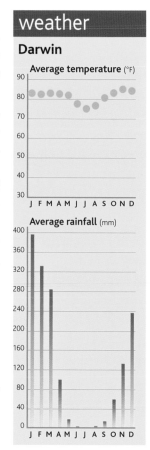

weather

Darwin

Average temperature (°F)

Average rainfall (mm)

Take Perth, for example, capital of Western Australia and the country's fourth largest city, where a high percentage of the city's 1,400,000 population is British. Sunny and fast-growing, it has a full hand of property, either in the city or its suburbs, or within commuting distance along forty miles of glorious coast or in the bush. If your budget were £250,000, you could consider a four-bedroom bungalow with pool on a quarter-acre plot in a suburb overlooking the Indian Ocean, or, fifty miles to the east, a four-bedroom house and small vineyard on ten acres, or large family properties with pools, on at least half-an-acre, within a half-hour commute or less.

If there is one generalization about Australian property, it is that architectural styles vary across the country according to climate changes. In Melbourne, where they are proud of their four seasons, houses reflect the weather, with plenty of brickwork and fireplaces. But in Queensland, houses are built to meet the demands of the tropical climate. They are more open-plan, often made of timber, and set high on wooden stilts.

points to consider

One of the most useful services provided by the Real Estate Institute for each Australian state (find their links from the national website at www.reiaustralia.com.au) is the up-to-date median price survey of local properties. Unlike average prices, which can be skewed by a cluster of unusually high or low prices, median prices are reckoned to be a more accurate reflection of true market activity. Median prices are the middle price in a series of recent sales, where half of the sales are of lower value and half of higher value. For example, if fifteen sales are recorded in, say, a city suburb, and arranged from lowest to highest value, the eighth sale price is the median price.

These median prices do *not* specify particular types of property. They are merely an accurate indicator of market activity in a particular area. It's up to you to decide whether you want to live in a waterside city high-rise, or a bungalow with a golden beach nearby or even a smallholding in the country with enough room for horses – and research the median price accordingly to determine whether you can afford it.

A quick glance shows that it is perfectly possible to buy a sizeable family home costing within £25,000 either side of the £125,000 mark. As a rule of thumb, scale down the number of bedrooms for an increase in luxury and better location. It is also immediately obvious where the property hotspots are.

price bands

£50,000–£100,000
- two-bed apt in Hobart CBD, Tasmania
- three-bed house in average Melbourne suburb
- one or two-bed off-plan apt, shared pool, Perth
- three-bed bungalow, Cairns estate, north Queensland

£100,000–£150,000
- three-bed house on NSW golf course development
- three-bed townhouse in Victoria state

- two-bed house in coastal town Western Australia
- two-bed bungalow, pool, conservatory, on Queensland coast

£150,000–£200,000
- one-bed luxury off-plan apt in New Quay docklands, Melbourne
- three-bed wooden house, two verandas, garden etc nr NSW coast
- five-bed nineteenth-century house in central Hobart
- three-bed timber house on stilts in four acres, NSW national park

£200,000–£250,000
- three-bed new house in smart Perth suburb
- four-bed house on South Coast development
- four-bed house in Melbourne suburb
- three-bed house in north Queensland rainforest

£250,000+
- luxury city apts, great views
- colonial country houses, extensive land
- big houses in smart city suburbs
- country estates, house and outbuildings

Buying property in Australia Q&A

Q How do I find an estate agent?

A Finding an estate agent is done just as it is in the UK via the Internet, local newspapers, property magazines, For Sale/Sold signs and their local offices. When dealing with an agent make sure they are a licensed member of the Real Estate Institute of Australia or one of the State based Real Estate Institutes. Visit www.reiaustralia.com.au where member agents and a number of property magazines are listed as well as links to their websites in the different states.

Outside the town of Mossman lie North Queensland's sugar cane plantations and the Daintree Wilderness National Park.

Q Are there any restrictions on a UK resident wanting to buy a property in Oz?

A Non-residents are not encouraged to buy property and need to acquire foreign investment approval from the Foreign Investment Review Board. Foreign residents can in most circumstances purchase a new house, home unit or vacant

Sydney has a great variety of architectural styles ranging from Victorian to Federation to the ultra-modern of the twenty-first century.

land, but there are restrictions. Visit www.firb.gov.au for details. If you are determined, seek the advice of a solicitor specializing in Australian property law. However if you have successfully applied for permanent residency, then the full range of properties is available to you.

Q What is strata living?

A A strata scheme is a building or collection of buildings where individuals own a separate part (e.g. a flat or a town house) with common property such as gardens, pool, external walls, paths. The common parts are the responsibility of the owners' corporation that also ensure the rules associated with living in the scheme are kept. If you are considering buying into a strata scheme, look at, or ask your solicitor to look at, the records of the owners' corporation and make sure you assess the general condition of the building and what repairs may need to be made. It is common to obtain a building inspection report and most real estate agents can recommend a local licensed person to do that for you.

Q What happens once I've found a property I like?

A The laws regarding real estate transactions vary slightly from state to state. The REIA website (see above) has links to the websites of its affiliate branches in the different states, each of which contains detailed information and advice on house-buying procedures. In general, the process is straightforward. Once an offer has been made and accepted, a contract is produced by the estate agent for signature by both parties. The point when you receive the contract is the point at which to involve your solicitor. S/he will advise you on the conditions of sale and make sure any conditions are included that you may want: for example, you may want to make the sale dependent on your getting a mortgage, the owner carrying out certain repairs and so on. A number of points are usually included in the contract:

- full details of the property, the terms of sale and of both the buyer and seller;
- the date of 'settlement' or completion, usually four to six weeks later;
- an agreed cooling-off period allowing time (two to five working days) to give the buyer the opportunity to withdraw; some sellers will insist that this clause is waived;
- fixtures and fittings;
- conditional clauses making the agreement subject to pest (white ants) and building inspections;
- if there are any defects in the property they should be mentioned as well as whether or not the seller is going to rectify them;
- other conditional clauses particular to the sale.

A deposit of 10 per cent is usually paid on signature and placed in the agent's escrow account until the date of settlement. If you unlawfully renege on the contract and pull out of the sale, you will forfeit the deposit.

The conveyancing procedure can be undertaken by your solicitor or a conveyancing or settlement agent (in Queensland it must be done by a solicitor) – a settlement agent is usually cheaper than a solicitor. Such an agent should be licensed by the Settlement Agents Supervisory Board and have a current triennial certificate. They will check there is clear title on the property, register the title, and undertake all local searches to ensure the property does not come encumbered with debts and has all the relevant certificates. NB: the states do slightly differ from one another in their conveyancing laws and requirements. There is no set fee for conveyancing a property, so shop around to find the best rate, making sure you know exactly what is included in it.

Settlement occurs when the buyer pays the balance of the purchase price, with adjustments for water and council rates, strata levies for apartments and any outstanding mortgages are paid off by the seller. The government issues either a certificate of title or a strata title, depending on the property.

Q What if the property is sold at auction?

A Selling property at auction is popular in Australia at all levels of the marketplace. Again, auctions vary from state to state and you should do your homework carefully before entering one, but there are some general principles to observe. Visit other auctions so you know the ropes and have seen what prices are reached; study the market in the area thoroughly, comparing the prices of like properties, and see what sort of price this one should be expected to go for; get hold of the contract before the auction so you can check what the property includes and the conditions of sale; make sure you have seen a building report and pest report; check your budget and keep it in mind while bidding; make sure your funds are in place. If you are worried about the excitement of the moment carrying you away, ask someone else to do the bidding for you. When the hammer falls on an offer, that's it. A minimum deposit of 10 per cent is payable immediately and there is no cooling-off period or going back.

Q What are the additional costs?

A Additional expenses vary between states but are likely to be 4–5 per cent of the purchase price and to include:

- solicitor's/conveyancing agent's fees
- survey and building certificate
- building inspection and pest report
- stamp duty
- land transfer registration fee
- mortgage registration fee
- mortgage discharge fee

If you have taken out a mortgage, there will be associated costs to factor in, occasionally including the loan application fee (about $600), stamp duty (0.4 per cent above $16,000), mortgage insurance if you've borrowed over 80 per cent of the purchase price (1 per cent of purchase price), ongoing lender fees.

Q Can I buy 'off-plan'?

A In Australia, it is known as buying 'off the plan'. If you decide to buy this way, there are a number of factors to consider. The contract should be carefully checked and legal advice taken on any benefits or restrictions. Ascertain whether you can make changes to the kitchen or bathroom, whether you can select appliances or choose the finishes, whether you can visit the site during construction. Check whether or not a certificate of insurance should be attached to the contract. There are times when the developer is exempted from doing this – your solicitor should be able to advise you. It's not always possible to know exactly what the finished unit will be like so try and be as specific as you can in terms of tying down the exact fixtures, fittings and finishes. Sometimes amendments are made to the building plans during construction. Try to ensure you are covered against this happening. Check whether any long-term agreements with caretakers or building managers have been entered into by the owners' corporation. If so, make sure you are happy with them.

Q Do I need a visa?

A Everyone travelling to Australia from the UK needs a visa.

If you are visiting on holiday, perhaps house hunting, you can get an ETA (Electronic Travel Authority) at the same time as you book your tickets. This has all but replaced the old visitor's visa.

For visits longer than three months, a temporary residence visa is required. There are twenty different categories of temporary residence visa which concentrate on the areas of skilled employment, cultural, social and international relations. Any applicant will also have to undergo a health and character check. Generally, if your application for a temporary residence visa is successful, you will be granted a multiple entry visa for the length of time you are staying in the country.

Once a mining town, Katoomba has become the popular, cosmopolitan capital of the Blue Mountains.

For permanent migrants, the best starting point is to visit www.immi.gov.au where you will find a number of downloadable booklets available that explain the different visas – partner, child, parent, other family, employment sponsored, general skilled, business skills entry and special migration – and the steps to take when applying to migrate to Australia.

In brief: To qualify for a visa, you must meet both the relevant personal and occupational requirements as well as being of good health and character. You will also have to prove you have the financial means to cover your travel and settling in to your new home. About half the migrants entering Australia do so under one of the various family visas. However, the government is anxious to encourage people who can plug holes in the job market by offering specialist skills, thus enlarging and improving the Australian labour force. A points scheme is used to assess whether

or not you meet the criteria which are based on age, experience, skills and language ability. Each criterion merits a certain number of points and you will need to amass enough to reach the Pass Mark. This is subject to change, so you will need to check when applying. There is a Pool where applicants who almost reach the pass mark are kept for two years but the chances of being accepted as a migrant to Australia are very slim. For more information visit www.immi.gov.au or www.australia.org.uk.

Q Are there any restrictions if I want to retire to Australia?

A In the first instance you should apply for a Temporary Residence Retirement Visa. This extends for four years and can be extended in two-year increments after that. You should be at least fifty-five, have no intention of getting employment, with only your spouse as a dependent, and be of good health and character. You must also be able to support yourself and partner financially and prove that you have capital for transfer of a minimum of $650,000A or a combination of $200,000A plus a pension/income/further capital providing income of a minimum of $45,000A per year. Approval of this visa takes between three to six months and costs $155A.

Q Should I use a migration agent?

A It is not necessary to use one but if you decide you would prefer to, make sure they are registered. This means they have to abide by the Migration Agents Code of Conduct and will charge for their services. If you are unsure about the points test, they will advise you about how to get your maximum number of points. A list of registered agents can be found at www.themara.com.au.

Rockhampton, in central Queensland, is the beef capital of Australia. Its elegant city centre contains restored nineteenth-century buildings and glorious Botanic Gardens.

Living in Australia

government and economy

Australia's government is three-tiered: federal, state and local. The Parliament has two chambers, the House of Representatives (Lower House) and the Senate (Upper House), both of which are democratically elected. The Queen appoints the Governor-General (on the advice of the Australian government) who acts on the advice of the ministers. The real political power however is held by the prime minister (www.pm.gov.au), and the government is run on the model of Westminster. The federal government's principal responsibilities include foreign relations, trade, defence and immigration. National elections are held within three years of a new meeting of a federal parliament, usually when the Governor General agrees to the request of the prime minister. Like the USA, Australia does have a written constitution that defines the role of the federal government

The state parliaments are responsible for legislating principally on education, transport, health, agriculture and law enforcement. Except for Queensland, the state parliaments have two democratically elected Houses, the Legislative Assembly (or House of Assembly) and the Legislative Council.

The local governments answer to the state governments. Their responsibilities lie closest to home and include town planning, transport systems, road construction and maintenance, weights and measures, public amenities etc.

Australia has a prosperous economy, its vast natural resources making it one of the richest countries in the world. It produces an enormous number of metals

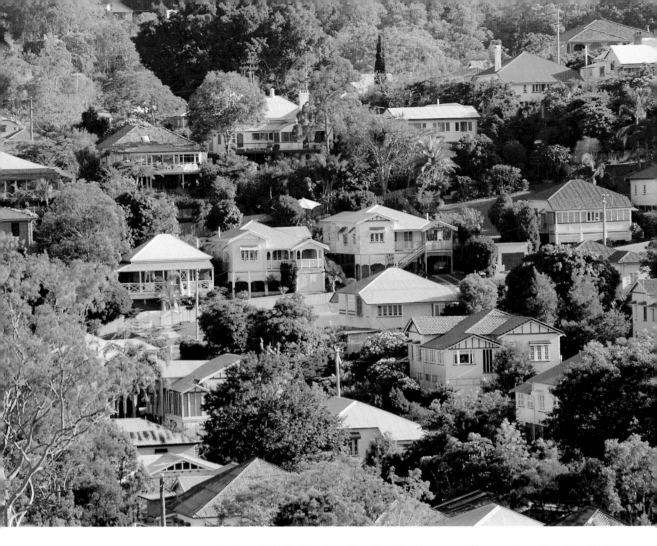

and minerals including bauxite, alumina, iron ore, diamonds and coal, gold, silver and other precious minerals. Mining takes place all over the country. Agriculture is another source of wealth, contributing 3 per cent to the gross domestic product (GDP), most particularly from wool, dairy production, cereals, sugar and fruit. The manufacturing industry is growing and with it the export of machinery and transport equipment. Plenty of small businesses contribute to this area, particularly in the areas of motor vehicles, aerospace engineering, chemicals, iron and steel, food processing and forestry. Although Australia numbers crude oil among its imports, it does produce natural gas while electricity is produced in coal-fired power stations. Rivers in the Snowy Mountains and in Tasmania generate hydroelectricity.

education

Educational standards are high in Australia with about 70 per cent of Australian children enjoying government-funded state education. There is a well-subscribed private sector that follows the same lines although it is possible in some private schools to take the International Baccalauréat in the final two years. The school year generally runs from roughly the end of January to December with four ten-week terms and no half-terms.

Education is compulsory from ages five to fifteen although it is available for twelve years. Preschools exist for four and five year-olds where the emphasis is on creativity and thinking, not reading and writing. In the year the child becomes six, s/he moves into primary school. Each state favours slightly different emphases but all focus on English, maths, social studies, health and physical education. Secondary education, beginning at age eleven (twelve or thirteen in WA) takes place at high school, either comprehensive or grammar. School Leaving Certificates (GCSE equivalents) are issued at the end of the tenth school year. The majority of pupils stay on to complete the final two school years, studying five to seven subjects, at the end of which they take public examinations (Tertiary Entrance Exam or Higher School Certificate) to qualify for tertiary education.

health care

Hospitals and medical practitioners in Australia meet the highest standards. They operate under a state-funded system and also privately.

Medicare is Australia's publicly funded health system affording treatment by doctors and hospital for all residents as well as tourists from countries, such as the UK, that have a reciprocal arrangement with Australia. Like the NHS, it provides free or subsidized health care and free hospital treatment. To join Medicare or to assess your eligibility, you should apply to one of their offices or call 13-2011 asking for an application form and the Welcome to Medicare booklet that will explain the services and how to get them. Once you've completed the form and supplied the appropriate documentation, you will be sent a Medicare card, giving your membership number, the names of family members also entitled to use the service and an expiry date. You will have to replace the card in five years. This card and the number is essential for making a claim or for receiving free treatment. NB: Foreign retirees with a temporary visa are not covered and should take out private insurance.

The benefit of taking out private insurance is the knowledge that you will be able to receive the treatment you need without delay usually with the specialist of your choice.

pensions

Until 2001, UK citizens making a new life for themselves in Australia could use their UK pension contributions to help qualify for an Australian pension. However on 1 March 2001, the Social Security agreement that existed between Australia and the UK was terminated. Now, UK citizens have to have ten years qualifying residence before being eligible to claim the Australian Age pension. Visit www.facs.gov.au/uk for further information.

If, when you move, you are already in receipt of a British pension, it will be frozen, i.e. you will not benefit from annual index-linked increments. For further information, visit www.dss.gov.uk. Transferring payment of your pension is straightforward. Inform your local DWP office and they will make appropriate arrangements to have your pension paid either by cheque or directly into your bank account. Tax is not payable on your pension. If you have not retired, it is worth completing a BR19 from the DWP to receive a Retirement Pension Forecast. It may help you plan your finances better.

pets

Pets are allowed into Australia subject to certain regulations. Your pet must be over twelve weeks old and microchipped. You will need to apply to the Australian Quarantine and Inspection Service for an import permit by sending the application form to the relevant quarantine station. Once your application is approved, you will receive a permit and two veterinary certificates that will need to be completed by a government authorized vet (LVI) who will give your pet the appropriate injections ready for export. Travel arrangements must be made with any airline provided the pet travels as manifested cargo in an International Air Transport Association (IATA) approved container and lands at Mascot, Sydney; Tullamarine, Melbourne; or Perth. It must travel with the import permit, Veterinary Certificates A and B, blood test results and vaccination records. On arrival, your pet will go straight to the quarantine station for thirty days. You will be responsible for all fees associated with its quarantine. For more detailed information visit www.aqis.gov.au.

driving

Australians drive right-hand drive cars on the left-hand side of the road. The wearing of seatbelts is compulsory. Using handheld mobile telephones while driving is against the law. An international driving licence is acceptable but permanent residents should acquire an Australian driving licence as soon as they take up residence. This will involve taking written and practical tests and, depending on the state, an eye test. There are variations on the highway code from state to state. General speed limits are 100/110kmph on national highways and 60 kmph in built-up areas. International road signs are used with distances in kilometres.

car

If you are considering taking your car to Australia permanently, bear in mind the cost. It is usually more cost effective to sell your car in the UK and buy new. However if you're hell bent on taking it with you, you must obtain a Vehicle Import Approval from the Vehicle Safety Standards Branch of the Department of Transport and Regional Services (02) 2674 7506 email Vimports@dotars.gov.au. Before leaving the UK, make sure you have checked that your vehicle conforms with the relevant state or territory registration requirements. It must meet the safety and emissions standards expected of vehicles on Australian roads. If it doesn't, you will have to modify the vehicle so it does. You will also be liable to pay customs duty, Goods and Services Tax and Luxury Car Tax (if applicable) at the port of entry. These taxes vary

so it is wise to check what they are before you ship your car. Visit www.customs.gov.au for guidelines. On arrival in Australia, the car will have to be steam-cleaned and inspected by the quarantine authorities who will issue a quarantine clearance. Next it will have to be checked for its roadworthiness, then registered with the local traffic authority on production of the relevant documentation.

Woy Woy is a holiday and retirement centre just 85 kilometres north of Sydney adjacent to the Brisbane Water National Park.

Temporary residents can bring a car (plus trailer or caravan) into Australia for up to twelve months without paying duty on them, provided they are exported from the country when their time is up.

taxes

The tax year runs from 1 July to 30 June with budgets being announced in May. All residents must have a tax file number that can be applied for from the post office or Taxation Office. Income tax is levied on a PAYE basis with provisional income tax payable by anyone who is self-employed or on a private income; it is calculated on the previous year's earnings and paid in advance. The lowest tax rate is 17 per cent on earnings over $6,000 rising to the highest rate of 47 per cent. Simply, the more you earn, the more you pay. Permanent residents are taxed on their worldwide income. Income tax returns are the responsibility of the individual. The government provides Tax Packs containing forms and a magazine to help clarify the process. Because Britain has a double taxation agreement with Australia, temporary residents are protected from having to pay tax in both countries.

Capital gains tax is payable on investment property only and on appropriate personal income tax scales. It is not payable on any gain made from the sale of a principle place of residents.

For further information, visit www.ato.gov.au or www.inlandrevenue.gov.uk.

House-hunters

New South Wales

Dave and Eileen Evans
Budget: £95,000

Above: Bateman's Bay. Four-bedroom bungalow in brand new estate with two bathrooms, living room and kitchen; small garden: £98,000.

Below: Tilba Valley. Traditional Australian homestead with three bedrooms, two bathrooms, kitchen, living room and large terrace; seven acres of land: £93,000.

Three years earlier, retired lecturer Dave Evans and his wife Eileen visited friends in Australia and fell in love with the country. To celebrate their fortieth wedding anniversary, they decided to buy a retirement home on Australia's south coast. Eileen was keen on a large garden while Dave was looking forward to the fishing, swimming, boating and low cost of living.

They started their search in **Bateman's Bay**, the nearest coastal town to Canberra. An old fishing town, it has four beaches within minutes of the centre and is known for its high concentration of new developments. Without a residents visa, Dave and Eileen were restricted to buying a new property so they visited a show home on a brand new development. Light, white and spacious inside, it had a large living and dining area, a long kitchen with granite worktops and a large family room. The main bedroom had huge windows plus en suite bathroom. 'It's a lovely looking house, nicely made and welcoming. We love the way the natural light floods through it.' Their house would be one of a projected 200 and would be completed within a year, giving Dave and Eileen time to organize their move from the UK. To their relief there was a 'sunset clause' in the contract guaranteeing their money back if the house was not completed within three months of the agreed date. They were also reassured to know that the developers had been in business for forty years with 400 developments in New South Wales.

Next they explored the **Tilba Valley** countryside, a quiet place with fields of cows and a National Trust village dating back to the 1880s. There are plenty of older rural properties here, among them a traditional homestead with seven acres of land. The modern decoration of the light open-plan living area and kitchen contrasted with the country feel of the master bedroom. The elegant bathroom was tiled in grey and had an unusual sunken bath. The interior had all been designed to take advantage of the great views. All this and ten minutes from the coast. The owners were downsizing and hoped to negotiate over some of the furniture, suggesting a price of £2,000. Dave and Eileen liked the idea of saving money by not having to ship so much from the UK. Eileen thought that she might landscape and cultivate a couple of acres, leaving the rest to nature. They were also happy to continue an arrangement with a neighbouring farmer who grazed twenty cows a day on the land in exchange for timber. Ultimately, however, they felt it was too much to take on.

They continued their search in the small coastal town of **Merimbula**, a comfortable, affluent place popular with English and Scottish retirees. Here Dave and Eileen saw an impressive twenty-one-year-old beach-front villa. The owners had recently spent £20,000 on renovations. Inside, the rooms were arranged on one floor with the large living area as the focus. It had polished wooden floors and three sets of French windows. A modern fitted kitchen with a granite-topped breakfast bar and tiled floors took up one corner of the room and led to a dining area with a decorative fireplace. The two double bedrooms had fitted wardrobes and glass doors out onto the terrace. The property came with a laundry room and a study that could also be used as a third bedroom. Outside the terrace wrapped around three quarters of the house, with a sheltered patio area built above the large double garage. Because the house had been built on a raised platform the terrace benefited from wonderful sea-views. Eileen was also interested in the local gardening club that boasted eighty members and a membership fee of £2 a year. Much as they liked it, they felt the house was too small.

Above: Merimbula. Three-bedroom renovated house with new roof, kitchen and outside terrace; double garage and small garden: £95,000.

Below: Narooma. Three-bedroom luxury villa with two bathrooms, kitchen, living room, store room and double garage; courtyard BBQ area, large veranda and stunning golf-course views: £131,000.

They finally visited the laid-back village of **Narooma** surrounded on three sides by the ocean. The best new development was right on the golf complex where a luxury house awaited. The large cream open-plan living room took advantage of stunning views across the golf course. The bright and practical kitchen had New South Wales hardwood floors. The BBQ courtyard was an essential part of Australian living. The disadvantages of living on a complex are the potential restrictions. In this case, residents could not park on the lawn, erect an awning without permission or change the external paint colour without the permission of the annual residents' meeting. A bonus was free five-year membership of the golf club but for Eileen the garden was too small, taken over by the golf course.

Having seen the properties, Dave and Eileen decided they definitely wanted to buy a retirement home in Australia. They planned to go for a new build with a larger plot than the one they had seen. Eventually after holidaying with friends who live in Perth, West Australia, they decided to look for a home on the west coast and are currently negotiating for an acre of ground in Mandurah, hoping their retired person's permit will encompass them buying two bungalows with a view to letting one of them.

House-hunters

Perth, West Australia

Sean Clarke and Mette Wendler
Budget: £120,000

Sean Clarke and his girlfriend Mette Wendler were following a long trail of emigrants from the UK to Australia. Business analyst, Mette, had applied for a job in Perth via videoconferencing calls (to be confirmed by a final interview

when she arrived in Perth) while Sean had decided to run his telecoms company, Calls4Business, from the other side of the world where they originally met on a backpacking holiday. Mette was eager to leave Birmingham. 'The architecture's ugly, the traffic's horrendous and the weather's awful.' So it was off to Perth where one in eight of the 1.4 million population is British, the cost of living is half what it is in London and nine out of ten people granted residency find a job within six months. Most people want to live on the coast but property there was beyond Sean and Mette's budget. Inland, the scenery quickly turns to bush and a family home with nine acres of land could be bought for around £100,000. This couple's dream home would have three or four bedrooms, office space for Sean, plenty of room for their dog and potentially for a horse and all

Above; Northern suburbs. Five minutes from the ocean; four-bedroom home with four large reception rooms; garden and pool: £120,000.

within a forty-five minute commute to Mette's office in the city.

First they visited the **northern suburbs** where most properties are bungalows built on small plots and prices have risen 20 per cent over the last year or so. Here they found a four-bedroom home with an open-plan family room and kitchen with space for a breakfast bar. But Mette was not keen on the amount of exposed brickwork. The games room was big enough to hold a billiards table, a pinball machine and a games machine. The simple white living room was complemented by a small dining room. The blue master bedroom had an en suite bathroom with a large corner bath. Outside, there was a 'boutique' pool with an in-built current to swim against. It was pointed out to the couple that it is the land rather than the property that appreciates in value here so while they would get a return on their money if they just gave the place a lick of paint, more substantial renovation was unlikely to. In any event, Sean and Mette had made up their mind that it wasn't the place for them. It was too small and in need of too much work to make it conform to their taste.

Below: Avon Valley. Four-bedroom house with living room, kitchen/diner and two bathrooms; ten acres land including vineyard and outhouses: £110,000.

In the search for more land, they headed fifty miles east of Perth to the **Avon Valley**. Traditionally agricultural land, this area is becoming popular with city workers who want to get back to nature, own horses and even run hobby farms. Homes tend to be older and cheaper than on the coast with prices only increasing by a modest 10 per cent in the previous two years. The nearest town to the property they saw is Toodyay, one of WA's earliest settlements. Set back from the road, this property had the benefit of its own vineyard at the front of the house. The light-filled living room had amazing views over the surrounding land. The kitchen/dining room was again not to Mette's taste. The master bedroom had two sets of French windows to the outside where the amount of space, outside living area, spa pool and vineyard made it a good find. There was also a number of outdoor rooms devoted to wine production. As Sean was proposing to work from home, to some extent keeping UK hours, he could run the vineyard, buying the necessary equipment from the current owner for

£19,000. An alternative would be to sell the grapes on, making about £5,000 per year now increasing to £10,000 as the grapes matured. They were both bowled over by the place but sadly felt it was too far from the city for comfortable commuting.

Next, it was on to the **Perth Hills**, a fairly upmarket residential area in the north-east of Perth, less isolated than the Avon Valley. Various equestrian centres would provide stabling for a horse and it's only a forty-minute commute to the city. The fact that the houses are frequently set well back from the road is evidence of the residents' desire for privacy without forsaking civilization entirely. Property prices here had risen 20 per cent over the previous two years, making the average house price £100,000. The property Sean and Mette viewed was hidden from the street, surrounded by trees and bush. As she went round the house Mette noted ways to improve it, in particular livening up the formal blue dining room and replacing the kitchen worktops with granite. The large family room was extremely cosy with a fireplace for when the temperatures dropped to a chilly 16°C in the winter. The master bedroom was a welcoming yellow and had a 'fantastic' en suite bathroom, spacious and modern. They were both very taken with the property, thinking that they might clear the encroaching woodland round the house to open it out and make room for the possible addition of a pool.

Above: Perth Hills. Four-bedroom, two-bathroom house with office, living room, dining room, kitchen, family room; terrace, heated spa pool and one acre of land: £128,000.

Finally they visited **Darlington**, an area popular with British expats, where most of the homes are new builds. Here they saw a house that needed some work. It had a jarrah (local hardwood) floor throughout the ground floor with bright modern windows giving the place light. The modern white kitchen needed some upgrading. Upstairs was a vast games room and a number of dated patterned carpets in the bedrooms that would have to be changed. The master bedroom had good fitted wardrobes but no en suite. The existing bathroom needed updating. Outside, there was a spa and solar-heated pool. Although on paper the house was everything they'd asked for, they were disappointed by the layout and thoroughly disliked the sheds outside. The house was also located fifty metres away from the main Great Eastern Highway, the main route east from Perth, so all the 'road trains' thundered down the hills using their air brakes and it sounded as if they were right by the M6.

Below: Darlington. Recently modernized three-bedroom house with three reception rooms; pool, spa and three sheds: £130,000.

Ultimately, there was only one property they liked – the one in the Perth Hills. However after the show, they explored the area further and found another property, just a five-minute walk away, that they preferred. There was no major work to be done, although the kitchen needed replacing. There were no trees to clear and it had a large swimming pool. Sean and Mette moved in the middle of January 2004 and have been decorating ever since. In the past few months Mette has bought two horses and these are stabled at the top of the road, and they have also added another Rhodesian Ridgeback puppy called Nabali to the family. Life is certainly fantastic and they have had no regrets about making the move.

Ex-pat experience

Sydney

Derek and Julia Parker

Lecture tours of Australia provided the ideal opportunity for writers Derek and Julia Parker to explore the country and form a firm attachment to it. 'Whenever we left, we'd say to each other, "One day",' remembers Derek. 'But Julia had elderly parents whom we didn't want to leave behind. It was only when they'd shuffled off the mortal coil that we began to consider moving.'

By this time they had been to all the major cities and decided Perth was 'beautiful but with nothing to do', Adelaide and Melbourne were 'great', but it was Sydney's cultural scene that caught their imagination. It took about twelve months to get a retirement visa during which time they went against all advice and bought a house. 'We came out in March 2002 and rented for a month to experience what it might be like to live here and to explore the property market. Then we returned in June and were the first people to be shown this house. We fell in love with it immediately.' It is a pretty one-storey Federation house in the suburb of Mosman with a large bedroom, guest bedroom, two studies, a large lounge/dining room, kitchen and music room. They are on the north shore with a mere seven-minute drive to get to the Opera House.

To their dismay the Parkers learned that, under the terms of their visa, they could not work, although an immigration lawyer agreed with them that writing would not constitute employment since they weren't taking jobs from native Australians. Since their application, the law has changed to allow retirees twenty hours of work a week. They brought over both their car, a French Citroen, and their wire-haired fox terrier, Toorak. The only problem was with the car – it was held up by the removal company for four months, but after some argument the company refunded the cost of a hire car. The move itself was expensive but they had no problems getting their furniture over, hiring a sofa, garden furniture and beds until their own arrived. One of their friendly neighbours introduced herself with the loan of a dinner service and wine glasses.

The Parkers have found the cost of living in their favour. 'It's a joy to fill the car with petrol for $40A when it cost £40 back home. Our grocery bill that averaged £75 a week back home now amounts to $95A, or about £45.' The income tax levels are high but there is much less indirect taxation. Since they're not entitled to Medicare, they have had to take out the most comprehensive medical insurance they could find – but have found that this is much cheaper than the British equivalent.

Friends were easily made, largely through joining Friends of the Art Gallery, the Cultural centre in Mosman, the Society of Authors and PEN, and in Julia's case, Fitness First, where she goes three times a week. 'We've also been blessed with fantastic neighbours who, when we returned to the UK for a holiday, not only

'My only minor complaint was having to change the electric plugs on all our appliances. That was hell.'

sopped up the rain that had leaked into the house but actually cleaned our car! It hasn't been hard to meet people without having to thrust ourselves around.'

When they're not writing or going to the theatre and cinema, Derek and Julia indulge in watching TV. 'Australian terrestrial television is much less good than in the UK. The ABC is government-funded, and its income has been viciously cut over the past few years, so they don't have money for the sort of TV drama you get on the BBC. However, we do have cable, and watch lots of films as well as BBC World and UKTV. The one thing we miss is the loo paper from back home and Marks & Spencer's Indian meal for two – though that's made up for by our discovery of Cheezels – melt-in-the-mouth cheese nibbles. We send them home in exchange for our weekly *EastEnders* tape.'

Other than that, they have no faults to find. Derek has started a list of things that are wrong with Australia but so far he's found nothing to put on it. 'My only minor complaint was having to change the electric plugs on all our appliances. That was hell.' he remarks. 'But it's the same voltage so they do all work here.'

Neither Derek or Julia have any regrets at giving up the 'insupportable English winter for chains of days with blue skies and great light'. They continue to work during the week although suffer from the English disease – 'If it's good weather, we'd better get out – it might not be so fine tomorrow. But it always is.'

USA

Introduction

A fantastic diversity of landscapes offers itself to the visitor to the United States: the surfing beaches of the West Coast, vast expanses of desert, the spectacular Grand Canyon, the shimmering Great Lakes, National Parks that meet every description, historic villages of the North-Eastern states, the twenty-first-century cityscapes of New York, Los Angeles, Chicago and the rest.

Each of its cities has its own distinctive flavour, whether it's the hectic rush of Manhattan, the smart metropolitan dignity of Boston, Washington and Philadelphia, the musical traditions of New Orleans, the rambunctious nature of Chicago, the oil-rich cities of Dallas and Houston, glamorous Los Angeles and laid-back San Francisco – all of them containing aspects of the best and worst of city life.

The fourth largest country in the world, the United States does everything on a grand scale. Due to its size and varied topography, the climate varies widely. The sunshine coast of Florida enjoys mild dry winters with hot humid summers while in New England the weather is changeable with generally mild summers and chilly winters. The Southern states enjoy humid sticky summers that are relieved by the cool found in the mountains whereas in Texas the summers are roasting with a hurricane season coming behind that brings plenty of rain to the area around Houston in particular, while the winters are warmer than the rest of the country.

Although the United States is renowned for its fast food there is plenty of ethnic cuisine throughout the country. Specialities include: the beef of Texas; seafood in the coastal areas such as lobster in Maine, clam chowder in New England, blue crab from Chesapeake Bay; Cajun, Creole and soul food from the south; quality ingredients from natural resources composing the healthy Californian diet; the hearty dishes of the Mid-West that were brought by immigrant Swedes, Norwegians, Poles and Germans. Shopping is a big part of the American way of life with impressive shopping malls and outlet stores being a part of almost every major town.

Sports play a huge role in daily life, the three big ones being basketball, football and baseball. But it's not just spectator sports that excite the nation. The coasts provide every conceivable kind of watersport, with hiking and mountaineering featuring in many of the national parks and skiing in Colorado, California and Utah to name only a few. National festivals occur across the country. San Francisco sees in the Chinese New Year in spectacular fashion. Mardi Gras is perhaps celebrated most flamboyantly in New Orleans. Try the green beer that marks the St Patrick's Day Celebrations in New York, Boston and Chicago. Enjoy the pyrotechnics that accompany the Independence Day celebrations on 4 July. Come the fourth Thursday of November, the whole of the United States celebrates Thanksgiving with a traditional turkey dinner rounded off with pumpkin and pecan pie.

It's impossible to cover every American state in this introduction so the following necessarily brief guide will focus largely on the states visited so far by the TV series

facts

Capital: Washington DC

Area: 9,629,091 sq km

Highest point: Mt McKinley (6194 m)

Lowest point: Death Valley (86 m)

Coastline: 19,924 km

Population: 290,342,554

Currency: US dollar (USD)

Time zone: GMT –5-10 hours

Electricity: AC 110V

Weights and measures: Imperial; pint has 16 fl oz

Religions: Protestant, Roman Catholic, Jewish

Languages: English, Spanish

Government: Constitution-based Federal Republic

International dialling code: 00 1

National holiday: 4 July, Independence Day

Maine's Mount Desert Island has some of the most peaceful and varied landscape of the region – the perfect place for a peaceful hideaway.

A Place in the Sun, mentioning websites that will provide more information.

new england

The six states, Maine, Vermont, New Hampshire, Massachusetts, Connecticut and Rhode Island, that make up New England occupy the North-Eastern corner of the United States. Christened New England in 1614 by the explorer John Smith, European settlement began in earnest with the landing of the Pilgrims in 1640. Theirs was a maritime economy with shipbuilding, fishing and whaling high on the agenda eventually to be replaced by the twenty-first-century interests of computers, biotechnology, finance, insurance and tourism.

With the Appalachian mountains to the west, the landscape includes lush forests, fertile valleys, large swathes of farmland, pristine lakes and a shoreline that varies from the rocky coast of Maine to the long stretches of sand on Cape Cod. All six states have preserved their historic character, seen in the picturesque small towns with their prevalent white-steepled churches and clapboard houses plus plenty of sites of historic interest.

Boston is central to the New England experience. Built round the natural harbour at the mouth of the Charles River, it is a charming, vibrant city with culture and history in abundance as well as the culinary pleasures of seafood, Boston cream pie and Boston baked beans. Massachusetts state is known for its beaches especially at **Nantucket**, **Cape Cod** and **Martha's Vineyard**, its opportunities for whale watching and fishing, its historic towns of **Salem** and **Plymouth**, its charming villages where historic architecture has been protected.

Rhode Island is the smallest state in the USA with a pleasant shoreline backed by woodland with two principal cities, busy **Providence** and **Newport** with its impressive colonial architecture. Connecticut is memorable for its shoreline, the Connecticut River Valley and Lichfield Hills scattered with sleepy communities in contrast to the skyscrapers of its capital, **Hartford**. Vermont is noted not just for its beautiful villages but particularly for its brilliant show of leaves in the Fall. **Burlington**, on the banks of Lake Champlain, is its largest city while up in the mountains **Stowe** numbers among the many ski resorts. The White Mountains of New Hampshire contrast with its spectacular lakes region, its 18-mile coastline and the unique Great North Woods. Historic **Portsmouth** and **Concord** are its two major cities. Finally Maine, the largest of the six states, offers wilderness aplenty

with its northern areas covered by extensive forests and lakes. Its dramatic coastline sports various resort towns, particularly the capital, **Portland**, the historic **Kennebunks** and **Freeport**.

For more information, visit: www.mass-vacation.com – official site of the Massachusetts Office of Travel and Tourism; www.visitrhodeisland.com – official Rhode Island Tourism site; www.tourism.state.ct.us – official site of Connecticutt Tourism; www.travel-vermont.com – official Vermont tourism site; www.visitnh.gov – official site of the New Hampshire Division of Travel and Tourism Development; www.visitmaine.com – official site of the Maine office of Tourism.

Dream of relaxing on Maine's oceanfront with its rugged shores and picturesque New England villages.

florida

In 1513, the Spanish explorer Juan Ponce de León spotted land and named it after Pascua Florida, the Easter Festival of Flowers. The Spaniards formally ceded Florida to the United States in 1819 and it became a state in 1845. The landscape is generally flat, the gentle hills in the north falling towards the coastal plains while in the south lie central wetlands fringed by golden beaches with countless opportunities for diving, snorkelling and other water-oriented activities.

The highlights of Southern Florida include stylish **Miami** with its affluent residential districts of Coral Gables, Coconut Grove and Key Biscayne. To its north, lie the yachties' haven of **Fort Lauderdale**, **Boca Raton** with its strictly observed style of Mediterranean architecture, and glamorous **Palm Beach**. Further north lies the Space Coast, home to the country's space industry, which is surrounded by protected national parkland and wonderful beaches. **Daytona Beach** is still

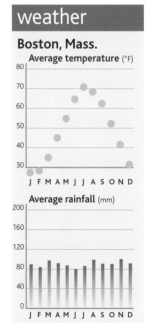

weather

Boston, Mass.
Average temperature (°F)

J F M A M J J A S O N D

Average rainfall (mm)

J F M A M J J A S O N D

focused on the pursuit of motoring thrills while **St Augustine** on the Treasure Coast is the oldest city in the state, offering an attractive historic centre and 43 miles of beach.

Once peaceful, rural farmland, central Florida has been overtaken by the advent of the theme park. Walt Disney World, Universal Studios, Sea World and Discovery Cove are major tourist attractions that bring thousands flocking to **Orlando** and its surrounds. Elsewhere, however, the old world lives on in towns like **Ocala** and **Mount Dora** or, further south, **Kissimee** where the area is known for its cattle ranches and orange groves.

The western Gulf Coast offers the most diverse range of experiences from the upbeat city of **Tampa** with its atmospheric Ybor City, the cultural pleasures of **Sarasota** and **St Petersburg** to the alligator-infested swamps of the Everglades National Park. The far south-west coast is one of Florida's best-kept secrets that is only now being developed. **Fort Myers** has a reputation as an up-and-coming town with laid-back **Naples** being the jewel in the Gulf Coast's crown.

Up in the north, the Panhandle has more in common with its neighbouring states of Alabama and

Tampa Bay is an upbeat waterfront area on Florida's West Coast that mixes an urban buzz in an attractive natural setting.

Georgia than with the rest of Florida. **Tallahassee** is the state capital although the biggest draw is the coast with its icing sugar sands. Inland, swamps, springs and savannahs are found in the unspoiled Apalachicola National Forest.

With its year-round sun, unspoilt beaches and excellent facilities, Florida presents the answer to almost everyone's dream.

For more information, visit: www.flausa.com – the State of Florida's official travel planning site; www.stateofflorida.com – useful information for moving to and living in Florida.

virginia

History is everywhere in Virginia with restored buildings or sites and places of historic interest dominant. The first British colony was established here in 1607. Prosperity was guaranteed by the tobacco trade until the mid-nineteenth century when it fell into decline. The death knell sounded for the state thanks to its involvement in the Civil War when it was ravaged by fighting.

Although laid to waste in the war, **Richmond**, the state capital, is now an elegant, thriving town where historic buildings mingle with those of the twenty-first century. Tree-lined avenues flanked by gracious post-Bellum mansions and brownstones contribute to the town's selection as one of the thirty American 'Most

Liveable Communities'. With easy access to Washington DC, mountains and the ocean, Richmond also offers plenty of shops, restaurants and entertainments.

Not far to the east, lies the Historic Triangle of **Jamestown**, **Williamsburg** and **Yorktown**. Here history can be revisited in detailed re-creations. You can also find the Busch Gardens, Williamsburg; the newly opened President's Park; Virginia's largest producing winery; musical theatre and numerous shopping opportunities. **Fredericksburg** is one of the prettiest towns in the state, its residential avenues divided by white picket fences. Once a significant port, its historic waterside buildings house antique and bookshops.

The Virginia coast is generally unspoilt with plenty of secluded coves. **Virginia Beach** is the most developed resort but remains low key while the appealing island of **Chincoteague** attracts fishermen, birdwatchers and beach bums.

To the west lie the **Blue Ridge Mountains** which, with the **Shenandoah Valley**, provide plenty of additional scope for outdoor activities as well as some of the most stunning natural scenery in the state. In the valley, small atmospheric towns have been restored to their historic glory and lie surrounded by horse farms and apple orchards. There's no doubt that if you're looking for America's past, Virginia is one of the most attractive places to find it.

Visit www.virginia.org for more tourist information or www.virginia.gov

One of Virginia's most attractive towns, Fredericksburg has an elegant downtown area with buildings dating back to colonial days.

tennessee

This most beautiful state divides neatly into three geographical regions: the great Smoky Mountains National Park, central Tennessee, the marshy Mississippi lowlands – each defined by their own distinctive music. People from all over the world flock to **Memphis**, home of the blues and birthplace of rock 'n' roll. The

websites

www.usembassy.org.uk – site of the US Embassy in London

www.whitehouse.gov – official site of the White House

www.visitusa.org.uk – comprehensive tourist site of Visit USA Association

Beale Street is the historic heartbeat of Memphis, the street that gave birth to the Blues. It still attracts visitors with its many musical venues and restored buildings.

weather

Louisville, Kentucky

Average temperature (°F)

80
70
60
50
40
30

J F M A M J J A S O N D

Average rainfall (mm)

200
160
120
80
40
0

J F M A M J J A S O N D

city was founded in 1819 and named after the ancient Egyptian capital on the Nile. Memphis was a keystone of the civil rights struggle and was where Martin Luther King was shot dead in 1968. After that, the city declined but has recently seen a striking upturn in its fortunes. The historic area of Beale Street, once renowned for its black culture, has been restored to include shops, cafés and clubs showcasing regional talent. One of the most famous properties in Memphis is Graceland, Elvis Presley's home for twenty years.

Principal town in the central plateau is **Nashville**, the country music capital of the world. First established as Fort Nashborough by European settlers in 1779, Nashville has developed into the financial and manufacturing centre of the mid-South and is home to numerous centres for higher education including Vanderbilt University. A replica of the Parthenon is testament to the city's nickname of 'Athens of the South' while its plethora of churches and church-related establishments gives rise to the tag 'Protestant Vatican'. South of the city, large plantation houses recall the state's past while the historic town of **Franklin** has some attractive buildings, **Shelbyville** is the focus for walking-horse shows and **Lynchburg** contains the unique Jack Daniels Distillery.

Until the establishment of the Smoky Mountains National Park in 1934 and the more recent construction of interstate highways, the eastern region of Tennessee remained cut off and untouched by time. It has spectacular countryside dominated by the mountains with sleepy towns scattered across the hills and valleys below. The National Park contains a huge variety of flora and fauna, including its renowned bears, and has plenty of hiking and cycling trails. Several tourist-driven towns thrive on the edge of the Park, including the dry town of **Pigeon Forge**, **Gatlinberg** and **Townsend**. Nearby **Knoxville** was once the state capital and boasts the University of Tennessee. The most famous town, thanks to band leader Glenn Miller, is picturesque **Chattanooga**. Set on a bend in the Tennessee River, it is surrounded on three sides by forested plateaux. Downtown Chattanooga is the lively reclaimed riverfront containing most of the town's main attractions, the Tennessee Aquarium and the Chattanooga regional History Museum among them.

Few Brits have moved to this part of the world, so you can be assured of a real escape from the UK to the hospitality of the deep South.

Visit www.tnvacation.com or www.state.tn.us, the official website of the state of Tennessee.

kentucky

Kentucky has plenty to offer from the mountains, plateaux and valleys of the south, through the gently rolling bluegrass of the heartland to the massive lakes and plains of the west.

In 1775, a treaty with the Cherokee allowed settlers from the East to move into Kentucky. In 1792, it became the fifteenth state to join the Union. The population were divided over slavery during the Civil War. Many plantation owners supported slavery, but the small farmers and mountain families did not. Kentucky was officially neutral during the Civil War only until September 1861 when it actively began support of the Union.

In nineteenth-century America, the Shakers lived communally. Their architecture is renowned for the governing principle of form following function. These houses are to be found in Kentucky.

weather

Houston, Texas

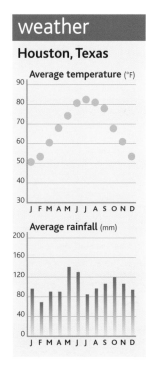

Average temperature (°F)

90
80
70
60
50
40
30

J F M A M J J A S O N D

Average rainfall (mm)

200
160
120
80
40
0

J F M A M J J A S O N D

America's thoroughbred horse farming is focused on the Bluegrass Downs. The hills are peppered with elegant houses, impressive barns and stud farms divided by typical plank fences. The largest town in the area is **Lexington**, home to the University of Kentucky. However the capital of the state is **Frankfort**, a country town that contains some impressive historic buildings, the Kentucky History Centre and the grave of Daniel Boone. To the south are the distinguished old towns of **Danville** and **Harrodsburg** with its historic Shaker village of Pleasant Hill. The eastern part of the state is dominated by the dramatic scenery of the Daniel Boone National Forest, visited by many who want to rock climb, boat, hunt, fish, ride and hike.

Laid-back **Louisville** is the cultural and industrial centre of rural Kentucky, renowned for its Kentucky Derby. It is also noted for the attractive parks that ring it as well as its thriving arts scene that centres on the Kentucky Centre for the Arts. South of the city there are various rural towns such as **Bardsville**, **Clermont**, both places to savour Kentucky bourbon, **Hodgenville**, birthplace of Abraham Lincoln, **Bowling Green**, home of West Kentucky University and **Elizabethtown**. Attractions in the area include My Old Kentucky Home State Park, Fort Knox (for the few minutes you're allowed to pull up and look), and the Mammoth Cave National Park with the most extensive underground cave system on earth. Western Kentucky has less to offer the dream-home buyer than the rest of the state. Small towns developed along the course of the River Ohio, notably **Owensboro** and **Paducah**, site of significant battles during the Civil War.

Visit www.kytourism.com for more information.

mississippi

One hundred miles of Mississippi coastline provides excellent white-sanded beaches and deep blue waters. Biloxi is its major resort.

During the eighteenth century, the French and Spanish laid claim to the area until it came under US control in 1796, joining the Union in 1817. The mainstay of the region was cotton and, to farm it, the plantation owners needed slaves. The state quickly seceded in the Civil War and played a major part in the conflict resulting in the devastation of its economy. Agriculture remained important until well into the early twentieth century. The deep racial divide that has existed for years has diminished somewhat thanks to the civil rights movements in the Sixties.

Largely a rural state, it nonetheless has the attractions of deserted beaches and casinos Las Vegas style, antebellum plantation houses and haunting blues music. The state capital is **Jackson**, perched on a bluff above the Pearl River in the central plain. Similarly perched but over the Mississippi is **Natchez**, an attractive town with fine examples of antebellum architecture, many close to the downtown district.

The Mississippi Delta stretches from **Memphis** to the historic port of **Vicksberg**. Enormous efforts are made to prevent the plains flooding so the cotton can be grown. **Clarksdale**, **Greenville** and **Greenwood** are the principal towns in the area known for their affiliation to the blues and to the cotton industry.

The state's hundred-mile coastline possesses a different character with its white-sanded beaches, twelve resort casinos and championship golf courses (see www.gulfcoast.org). **Biloxi** is a neon-lit sprawl along the highway, its seafront used by floating casinos. However the shady tree-lined streets of **Old Biloxi** offer a more relaxed atmosphere. **Gulfport** is another casino resort while, in contrast, **Ocean Springs** is a friendly residential community.

See www.state.ms.us – the official state website of Mississippi

texas

The Spaniards who discovered Texas in 1519 named it Tejas from the Caddo Indian word for 'friend'. In 1821 it became a state of Mexico but the Texans fought vigorously for their independence until the Republic of Texas was formed, becoming the twenty-eighth state to be admitted into the Union.

Texas is an enormous state of vast geographical diversity. Much of the state is characterized by oil-rigs and cattle farms but for those looking for a holiday home, the Texan stretch of coast bordering the Gulf of Mexico offers numerous attractions. It has over 600 miles of glorious beaches and bird sanctuaries and has earned the nickname of the 'Third Coast'. **Houston,** Texas's largest city, is congested and diverse, its chief attractions lying south-west of downtown where the Menil Collection and the Museum of Fine Arts are to be found. The most popular area is the Montrose District with its opportunities for shopping, clubbing, eating, drinking and gallery going. Just outside town is the Johnson Space Centre.

The coast itself is heavily developed with condos. Although the climate varies from mild at Galveston to subtropical by the Mexican coast, there is always a wind to cool things down. **Galveston** has been rebuilt having been burned to the ground in 1821. Considerable restoration work has revived impressive Victorian mansions particularly those close to the Strand. Watch out for the exuberant Mardi Gras festivities. Top tourist attraction is Moody Gardens, an environmental research facility. The other resort town to single out is **Corpus Christi**, a commercial

The River Oaks neighbourhood of Houston, Texas was developed in 1924 as a model suburb that would influence the city planners.

Famously home of the old London Bridge, Arizona's Lake Havasu City is a popular destination for American second-home owners.

port town which is fast growing and is home to the Texas State Aquarium, its heritage Park and Museum of Science and History. The Padre Island National Seashore (www.nps.gov.pais) is one of the longest expanses of undeveloped coastline in the US and a popular holiday destination thanks to its boundless opportunities for outdoor activities.

See www.traveltex.com – the official site of Texas tourism.

arizona

On the border of Mexico, Arizona is known as one of the 'sunbelt states' where the sun beats down 300 days of the year. Its landscape is extreme with vast plains and jagged mountains and dramatic rock formations, the most notable of all being the Grand Canyon. Until the pioneers arrived in the late 1700s, Arizona was Indian country. 1886 saw the last stand of the Apache tribe and, in 1912, Arizona became the forty-eighth state of the Union.

Set in the Sonoran Desert Valley, **Tucson** has expanded without losing its historic quarters. Home to the University of Arizona and destination for many American retirees, it is surrounded by magnificent scenery and presents a mix of US and Mexican cultures.

Phoenix is the sixth largest city in the US and is still rapidly expanding, already having swallowed the nearby towns of Scottsdale, Mesa and Tempe. Surrounded by desert and reaching across the Salt River valley, it is a thriving metropolis tipped as a number one golfing destination and famed for its many health spas. Tourist attractions are few, numbering among them the Heard Museum and Taliesin West, Frank Lloyd Wright's studio. East of Phoenix lies a mountainous wooded area where the modest towns offer respite from the raging summer heat.

Central Arizona is spectacular Red Rock country dotted with Indian sites and old mining towns. **Prescott** was the first territorial capital, now boasting five lakes, six golf courses and plenty of nature trails as well as a well-preserved historic downtown complete with a strip of saloon bars. The former mining town of **Jerome** holds a precarious but impressive position on the side of a mountain, many of its residents making their living from arts, crafts and antique shops. Voted 'the most beautiful place in America' by *USA Weekend* magazine, **Sedona**'s main attraction lies not just in the awe-inspiring scenery but in the numerous locations where energy vortexes can be felt. This has attracted many residents in search of spiritual growth and renewal.

Navajo and **Hopi** Indian reservations dominate the north-east corner of the state, again blessed with breathtaking surroundings including the Canyon de Chelly.

See www.arizonaguide.com – official site of the Arizona Office of Tourism.

california

Discovered in 1542 by the Spaniards from Mexico, California wasn't colonized until the eighteenth century when various Catholic missions were set up to convert the natives and a number of forts to beat back the British and the French. In 1848, the USA took possession of California only days before the Gold Rush began and the population exploded. In 1850, California was admitted to the Union as a non-slave state. It is now the most populated state in the USA and a melting pot of numerous cultures.

The golden state of California now seems the epitome of everything American. At its heart lies big, brash **Los Angeles**, dominated by glamour, Hollywood, affluent mansions, sun-drenched beaches and money. But there are other facets to this particular diamond. The first Spanish mission was established where **San Diego** today stands on its fine natural harbour with a historic downtown and attractions such as Sea World and San Diego Zoo. Another renowned mission was the germ for red-roofed and white-walled **Santa Barbara**. Now popular with retirees, it is also home to five colleges, including the University of California. Further north still lies **San Francisco**, not far from Napa Valley, home to many wineries.

Inland in the south, lies desert country, inhospitable and awe-inspiring, fringed by the resort towns of **Palm Springs**, **Rancho Mirage** and **Indian Wells**. North of Death Valley National Park is Yosemite National Park, a wilderness of forests, rock formations, waterfalls and alpine meadows.

weather

Los Angeles, California

Average temperature (°F)

80
70
60
50
40
30

J F M A M J J A S O N D

Average rainfall (mm)

200
160
120
80
40
0

J F M A M J J A S O N D

Rows of vines characterize the rolling landscape of California's Napa Valley.

The attractions of California are legion, from modern metropolises and resorts to historic towns and small villages; from hiking and camping to mountain-biking, skiing and surfing; from redwood forests to sun-baked deserts; from the best in twenty-first-century arts and culture to a plethora of indigenous cuisines. There's something here to suit everyone.

See www.visitcalifornia.com – site of the California Division of Tourism.

The property market

For many years now, Florida, packed with tourist and leisure attractions, has been a favourite among Britons seeking a second home abroad. The Sunshine State has a thriving property market which, despite fears of a slump after September 11, continues to grow with billions of dollars pumped annually into new residential developments from the Atlantic coast to the Gulf of Mexico.

Thanks to the recent weak dollar, the sun has been shining even more brightly on UK buyers. Steady demand has turned into a mini-stampede, with Britons and other non-US citizens happy to buy outright or pay 25 per cent in cash and the balance on a US mortgage which some hope to service with rental income.

Favourable exchange rates, coupled with the notion that buying property in the USA is not such an alien concept as it once was, has led British buyers to turn their attention to other American states. Of course, there are relatively expensive

Bisbee, Arizona, has a balmy climate and rural setting that attracts those wanting an escape from the urban sprawl. It is an artistic community known for its antiques, galleries, community theatre and historic homes.

locations, such as California, which has been a popular holiday destination for a long time. But this new spirit of adventure is leading buyers to widen their horizons. They realize that there is more to the US than Walt Disney and golf, and that there are sunny bargains to be found in states such as Georgia, Arizona, Texas, Louisiana, Tennessee, Kentucky, Oklahoma and South Carolina. They can be a more enticing and cheaper alternative to pricey western Mediterranean hotspots.

American properties may appear to be bargains by our standards. But annual costs can be hiked up by extras such as high insurance, community association charges and even country club membership if that's where you intend to go for golf, tennis, swimming and the gym. Do the math, as Americans say.

types of property

As you would expect in such a vast country, there is an enormous variety of architectural styles, ranging from the kind of properties you see in the movies – ranches in cowboy country and plantation houses in the Deep South – to manor houses, Spanish hacienda-style properties, Art Deco glories, log cabins, city lofts, skyscrapers, concrete condos, contemporary Floridian-style holiday homes or Mediterranean-style villas.

Originally built in 1900 to resemble its Italian namesake, modern-day Venice, Los Angeles, retains some surviving canals, a world-famous beach and boardwalk.

One phrase you will hear again and again is 'cookie-cutter homes' – those acres of houses in suburbs and developments, perhaps with slight variation of size and shape, but all in the same basic style and many of them none the less attractive for that.

Land in the United States is generally cheap compared with that of Britain and many other Western countries where land values push up property costs. Widespread use of prefabrication also means that US building costs tend to be less. If a strict budget is important, Americans tend to sacrifice garden space for a bigger home. Families would rather have a large house surrounded by a comparatively small garden (albeit with outdoor living space – some of it probably covered – such as deck, barbecue pit and perhaps a pool) and depend on membership of a nearby country club for most outdoor recreation.

Consequently, American homes tend to be bigger than in other countries, especially away from towns and cities. The average size of a typical new family house in the USA is about 2,000 sq ft, which is roughly twice the size of its UK equivalent. As well as the various rooms you would expect in a detached UK home, the American house might have an extra family living room, double the kitchen space with all mod cons, extra large garage, a den (study), laundry room and so on.

In the tourist areas of sunbelt states, **Florida** especially, over three-quarters of UK buyers factor the rental market into their budget. A swimming pool is almost obligatory to go with their three- or four-bedroom home. Indeed, it is expected if the house is to be rented out for part of the year. So too is the lockable room, that vital space to store clothes and other personal items while the owner is away for much of the year. And air conditioning, of course.

One estimate puts the number of Britons living in Florida at 50,000, with 70 per cent of them in Orlando, the world's number one tourist destination at the centre of almost one hundred theme parks and other major attractions, as well as golf courses and wildlife conservation areas. Chances are that anything you buy here, if you are not the first owner, will have been built in the past couple of decades,

And with new developments springing up near Orlando and elsewhere throughout the state, the Florida buyer is spoilt for choice. Some developments are exclusively for over fifty-five-year-old retirees (e.g. The Villages, less than fifty miles from Orlando). And of course some areas are pricier than others (e.g. on the coast, especially, and very big bucks indeed for older waterside properties on the Florida Keys or the colourful Art Deco homes on Miami's South Beach).

But in the main, particularly inland where there is plenty of land and new developments flourish, Florida property prices remain reasonable despite their sought-after location. In the Sunshine State, for the price of a two-bedroom semi in a UK Midlands suburb, you could buy a four-bedroom detached house, plus pool and two-car garage.

Those wishing to leave Disney behind and explore nearby states have discovered **Georgia** where, with the exception of prime beachside homes which can go for several million dollars, prices are even more favourable. Even so, a three-bedroom timber-framed Southern-style house and pool bought there for little more than £100,000 half-a-dozen years ago will have almost tripled in value by now. And a

Fort Walton Beach is one of the cities strung along Florida's Emerald Coast, affectionately known as 'Redneck Riviera'.

two-bedroom apartment in a condominium will have done almost as well. Both types of property attract rentals from American snowbirds from the northern states in the winter and from the British in the summer.

Bargain-hunters are also exploring **Texas** which is not all cowboy country. It boasts a desirable coastline stretching down to the Mexican border. Even though prices have been rising in recent years in property hotspots, from the cosmopolitan city of Corpus Christi to the exclusive resort of Rockport nearby, they remain below the national average. A fisherman's house on stilts or a modern seafront home along the hundreds of miles of sandy beach are affordable. But away from the coast, in cattle country, prices drop to almost half the national average. And properties such as single-storey prairie ranch-style houses and period homes (i.e. over fifty years old) can come with ample cheap land.

A feature of Texas is the Plantation House, or a more recent version of this architectural style. Genuine – and expensive – ones (think of *Gone with the Wind*) were built in the thirty years before the start of the American Civil War in 1861. It was essentially a Greek revival style, grand, symmetrical and boxy, with central entrances, balconies, columns and pillars. There have since been many variations on this theme, and not so pricey as they look.

Plantation-style houses are found throughout the Southern states, where most types of property are cheap compared to the national average. States such as **North** and **South Carolina** and **Louisiana** are a bargain-hunter's paradise. And cheapest of all is **Oklahoma**. The obvious drawback is that they attract fewer people wishing to rent your property while you are not there.

Another state worth investigating is **Arizona**, where prices are still reasonable despite being pushed up thanks to its increasing popularity with Americans. The

Luxury homes and apartments line the pristine streets of Florida's Palm Beach, known for the sorts of property that only the very wealthy can afford.

varied landscape is host to a wide choice of affordable property, ranging from cookie-cutter homes plus pool in upmarket suburbs of Phoenix, the USA's sixth largest city, through Mexican-style haciendas in the desert to timber hunters' lodges in the mountains. Arizona is rich in tourist trails and attractions (the Grand Canyon, for example), has golf and skiing in abundance, so choose wisely and you will have a highly rentable second home.

California, well known to British tourists, is attractive to UK buyers, particularly those with deeper pockets. Not only is it a more expensive destination to travel to, property prices are about 25 per cent higher than Florida and in some areas – Orange County, Beverley Hills and smart enclaves in San Francisco – are among the highest in the United States. The price of a three-bedroom two-bathroom property in Florida might only buy a one-bedroom beach property in southern California. Rural California is a better bet for those with a limited budget.

Turning away from the sunbelt states, increasing numbers of Britons are looking to the New England region in the north-east US (**Connecticut**, **Maine**, **Massachusetts**, **New Hampshire**, **Rhode Island** and **Vermont**). Although many of the more attractive properties are holiday retreats for wealthy New Yorkers and Bostonians, it is possible to buy traditional two- or maybe three-bedroom clapboard houses for little over £220,000. A good example is the area around Lake Sunapee, an hour-and-a-half from Boston.

Of course, for those who love the rush of living in a vibrant city, **New York** is the magnet with the strongest pull. It can be expensive, depending on the architectural style and location, but if you have set your heart on a New York bolthole, you could find a small studio apartment for £125,000 and a reasonable one-bedroom apartment for double that.

points to consider

It is quite possible to rent out your property to help pay your mortgage. After all, at the time of writing, unless a special visa is granted, British tourists and homeowners can stay in the US for only six months of the year, with a maximum of twenty-eight days for one visit. If finance is an issue, and you are treating your American property as a lock-up-and-leave holiday home, there is little point in leaving it standing empty.

It might as well earn its keep. If your property is in the right location, for example an established holiday destination for Americans, it is reasonable to expect to cover annual costs with four months' rental income. Beware: if potential rental income is a factor, be careful where you buy. In some zones, short-term lets are forbidden, while in others they are restricted to certain months of the year. Try and get away with it and you could find your new neighbours informing the authorities. Local residents' committees, keen to protect their property investments, can keep a strict eye on other aspects of their communities – for example, not allowing owners to build extensions or paint the exterior of their houses a different colour without their permission.

The Painted Ladies are six much-photographed Victorian houses now dwarfed by the San Francisco skyline. Elsewhere in the city are other such houses waiting to be discovered.

In holiday areas, there are numerous rental agencies which, for a fee of 15–20 per cent of rental income, or more, bring in tenants, organize handovers and deal with day-to-day maintenance. You are partly paying for high standards expected by American renters. If you intend your American home to be primarily an investment, with your annual holiday(s) as a bonus and little more, one-stop-shopping could be the answer. Some estate agents offer so-called turnkey packages; they arrange your mortgage, sell you a fully furnished house – right down to the cutlery and bed linen, if you wish – and then manage the rental. All you have to do (apart from stump up the deposit and sign the mortgage papers) is turn the front door key and it's ready to go.

American renters fall into two categories. Either they are workers, who don't enjoy long holidays and therefore rent for short periods, sometimes just a week or even weekend; or they are snow-birds, for the most part elderly couples from the north who negotiate better rates to spend their winters in the sun.

Boston's Beacon Hill is an early nineteenth-century neighbourhood where the houses are well-maintained, the streets cobbled and lit with gas lighting.

As mentioned above, any weakening of the US dollar means that sterling-holders can buy cheaper, or bigger. Some astute investors at the receiving end of this bonus have sold their American home and traded up, reinvesting the profit in a better American property rather than converting their dollars back into sterling, which would have made no financial sense.

price bands

Below £100,000
- one or two-bed condo, community pool, e.g. Arizona
- small family home in Texas, prairie or town
- bargain family houses in Oklahoma
- cheap family foothold in Florida

£100,000–£150,000
- two-bed condo Georgia coast
- four-bed houses plus pool north or south Florida
- small New York studio apartment
- midwest family house, e.g. Minnesota

£150,000–£200,000
- three-bed modern house, pool etc., near Orlando, Florida
- new four-bed upmarket cookie-cutter in Phoenix suburb, Arizona
- large rural/desert/mountain family house in sunbelt state
- smallish New England clapboard house

£200,000–£250,000
- three-bed timber-frame Southern-style house plus pool, Georgia
- four-bed smart detached house, pool, Florida golf resort
- one-bed prime Californian beach property
- one-bed good New York apartment

£250,000+
- as before, but bigger (five-bed+), better and smarter location, e.g. beach or waterfront, mountain views, balconies, decks, pool, spa, acres of land in rural areas
- New York apartment (two bedrooms+)

Buying property in the USA Q&A

Pacific Grove, California or 'Butterfly Town USA', is situated at the tip of the Monterey Peninsula and is renowned for its down-home spirit.

Buying property in the USA is highly regulated and quite different from buying property in the UK so it is important you seek good independent advice to ensure you avoid any pitfalls. Try to find a suitable lawyer or realtor recommended by other expatriates and certainly shop around until satisfied with their terms and reputation.

Q Are there any restrictions on foreign ownership?
A None.

Q How is property sold in the USA?
A There is a central register of all properties for sale known as the MLS (multiple listing service) to which member realtors have access. The idea is to use one realtor in the area you like and with several different kinds available you need to be certain which responsibilities yours will shoulder. Do *not* sign anything that commits you to your realtor as this is unnecessary. A buyer's broker has a fiduciary duty to look after buyers even though the seller is responsible for payment of the sale fee.

weather

Miami, Florida

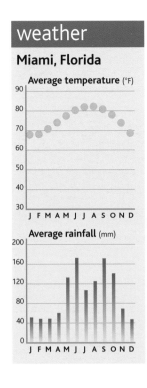

Average temperature (°F)

Average rainfall (mm)

You can view any number of properties for sale regardless of where the property instructions originate and if a purchase results with additional realtor involvement a split commission is arranged between them. Ask your prospective realtor if they hold a Real Estate Commission licence (REC). If they do, this will protect your interests because they are obliged to act under a code of conduct and you can be reimbursed if you suffer losses through their unprofessionalism.

Having selected a realtor or broker in your area, expect them to be far more involved in the process than a UK estate agent. They will show a buyer around various properties and then, once a property is chosen, they will submit the offer to the vendor's agent. If it is accepted, possibly after some negotiation on which they may advise, they will draw up a contract between the buyer and vendor subject to any conditions specified by the buyer such as being subject to survey, finance agreements, termite check (common on old properties) etc. Some conditions may be required by law; others will be suggested by your agent or lender. It will also state how the closing costs will be paid since they are a matter of negotiation. It should also state exactly what is being sold, whether any furniture, outbuildings and land are included. When the buyer is satisfied that the contract contains all the necessary conditions and clauses to protect him, ideally in consultation with an independent legal adviser, then he must sign and leave a deposit.

Q Are there any other considerations we should take into account?

Lively San Diego is set on a scenic curving bay, has forty-two miles of beaches and various parks and museums.

A While shopping around for the best mortgage deal or arranging your finances, buyers should be aware that owners' title insurance will be required to ensure against any future claim by a third party. It is also worthwhile taking legal advice at this stage on gift and inheritance tax and their implications. This necessarily requires advice about how you should title the property (in your own name, or jointly with your spouse, a trust or a company).

If buying a new property, ensure the building costs are paid and that the contract relating to your property and purchase has been approved by a lawyer qualified in US contracts.

There are many issues which can inadvertently lead to the loss of your deposit. Most of them are avoidable by simply asking the seller to modify certain clauses – unfortunately you will not necessarily know which clauses to change without the advice of a US lawyer, as some are not obvious.

It is impossible to deal here with every issue that may arise. What is important is that you do your homework, seek advice from independent realtors, other expatriates, your solicitor, the immigration

authorities and an experienced US financial/mortgage advisor before you make a purchase. But if you are scrupulously thorough and are clear about what you want, you will soon find yourself on the yellow brick road to your American dream.

Palm-lined streets, flanked by gingerbread mansions and tin-roofed conch houses typify Key West, the most southerly town of Florida.

Q Once we've found our dream home, what procedures do we have to follow?

A When the offer is accepted and finance obtained, the process is handed over to the closing agents or title company who are independently operated and are similar to an insurance company. Most real estate lawyers operate their own in-house title company. They ensure there is clear title to the property and the absence of any debts, restrictions or easements, e.g. rights of way. Just before completion, return to the property to check that everything is as it should be according to the contract. Now is the moment to ask the vendor to put anything right. The completion of the contract will be carried out in a meeting between the title company, the buyer and seller, the realtors, any lawyers involved and representatives of the mortgage company or bank. On signing the contract, the money will be transferred to the vendor and the keys handed over to the buyer.

The northernmost barrier island off the Florida coast, Amelia Island has thirteen miles of uncrowded beaches, world-class golf and top oceanfront resorts.

Q What are the implications of letting our property for part of the year?

A If, as a result of the restricted immigration laws, you decide like most non-residents to rent out the property you buy, it is vital to check the existing and planned regulations on short-term lets. For instance, many regions in Florida are zoned and short-term letting restrictions are common in many cities, communities or counties. In some places you may not be able to rent out your property at all and even when there is no zoning you will still need to consider implications if this were ever to change at a future date.

The reason for these restrictions is that many full-time residents object and hotels want a monopoly on short-term accommodation. Remember not every location will enable mortgage repayments to be covered by rental income and for this to occur besides choosing a suitable property and location, great care in your choice of management company will be required. It is unwise to rely on any future rental income to pay for a purchase as there can never be a foolproof guarantee.

It is essential always to obtain independent advice, particularly when the sales company provides their own management service as the two operations often conflict. Check especially for inflated rental projections and question any so-called 'guarantees'. If you rent out a property for more than fourteen days you must file a US tax return and pay tax on the income, although there is a US and UK tax treaty preventing double taxation and you can offset mortgage costs and travel expenses. Obtain specialist accountancy advice as this is essential.

As rental income is normally paid in dollars a fluctuating exchange rate should only impact on your deposit should you be fortunate enough to generate sufficient rental income to cover the purchase costs.

It is also important to ascertain if there are any community restrictions on a property. This may forbid you from hanging washing outside, prescribe the colour of the exterior and so on. Will living within their confines suit your lifestyle?

Q What additional costs should we allow for?

A You should expect additional charges to amount to approximately 5 per cent of the purchase price. These may include legal fees, the title search, title insurance surveyor's costs, homeowners' insurance and mortgage tax, although in the case of a new home the builder often contributes to these costs. Be prepared to pay property tax annually, the amount varies between 1 per cent and 3 per cent depending on the location of the property and is used to finance local services.

Q Do I need a visa?

A UK residents are currently part of the Visa Waiver Program that allows them to visit the States for a period of up to ninety days without a visa as long as they are travelling on a participating airline, hold a valid passport and an onward or return ticket to a country other than Canada.

Q What if I want to stay for longer?

A The United States has strict immigration laws. Before you buy a property, make sure you are eligible for the appropriate visa. The B1 and B2 visas are used for stays of up to six months. The B1 visa is required by people who are travelling on business. The restrictions on a B1 visa holder are considerable, basically prohibiting the holder from receiving any salary or reimbursement from a US employer. There are other temporary work visas available. The B2 visa is generally used by holidaymakers and holiday homeowners. Beware: if you

Across Boston's Charles River lies Cambridge and, most notably, Harvard University.

The heritage of Leesburg, Virginia, has been maintained in its faithfully restored historic buildings.

overstay the allocated time, the visa will be voided. If you overstay by more than 180 days, you will be barred from re-entering the country for three years. If you overstay for longer than a year, you will be barred for ten years.

An advantage of having either of these visas is that, once in the US, the holder can change to another non-immigrant status without having to leave the country provided the application is approved by the USCIS.

The visa question is extremely complex and liable to change, so for more detailed information visit the US Citizens and Immigration Services (USCIS) website at www.immigration.gov. Immigration lawyers exist to help you select and apply for the appropriate one.

Q Can I move there permanently?

A Permanent residence in the US is impossible without obtaining a 'green card' first. The card is in fact white these days. It contains microscopic portraits of all forty-two presidents, a hologram of the Statue of Liberty, representations of the state flags, a digital fingerprinting system plus an optical memory stripe, all of which enable the authorities to ascertain that it is the real thing. It is notoriously difficult to obtain one of these cards. Start by visiting the USCIS website (see page70) where the various types of eligibility are explained. Many people employ expert help to guide them through the maze of paperwork involved. Obtaining a green card does mean that you can officially work in the US but it also means that you must make it your new home. If you don't, you run the risk of losing the card. Once you have owned one for five years, you can apply for citizenship.

Living in the USA

government and economy

The United States of America is a federal republic made up of fifty states and the federal district of Washington DC. The government operates under a two-party system of Democrats and Republicans and is based on the Constitution of 1787. The division of power is between three branches – the executive, the legislature and the judiciary – each democratically elected and functioning independently. The executive branch is headed by the President and is responsible for administering the laws passed by Congress. The president is democratically elected, holds office for a four-year term and can be re-elected once. His power is limited by Congress, responsible for making laws. Congress is made up of the Senate (two senators per state) and the House of Representatives (435 members representing the electoral districts).

To a certain extent, each state controls its own affairs under an elected governor. They may set their own taxes and draft local laws affecting education, health, trade, state highways, highway code, criminal justice and so on. Each state is made up of counties, municipalities, towns and school or special districts that have their own local government administered by a mayor and his council responsible for grass-roots concerns such as police, fire and ambulance, public parks, waste disposal etc. Visit www.firstgov.gov – the official gateway to all government information.

Portsmouth, Virginia, is known for its many period homes built in a wide range of architectural styles.

The USA is the leading industrial power in the world, highly diversified and technologically advanced. Its principal areas of production are petroleum, steel, motor vehicles, aerospace, telecommunications, chemicals, electronics, food processing, consumer goods, lumber and mining.

education

Just as in the UK, state education can be uneven and has a bad reputation. It is possible that even as a permanent resident, you may not be able to take part in it. In which case the only option is to turn to private school. Non-compulsory pre-school

education exists for children aged two to five. Elementary school is for children aged five to eleven where they are taught the basic three Rs, plus history, geography, science, art, music, crafts and PE. Foreign languages are taught in some states. Secondary school lasts from twelve to eighteen, each year known by the following: Freshman (age fourteen to fifteen); Sophomore (fifteen to sixteen); Junior (sixteen to seventeen) and Senior (seventeen to eighteen). At the end of the senior year, the pupil receives a high school diploma having also taken national college aptitude tests during the last two years There are a number of guides to independent schools but visiting www.nais.org is a good start.

health care

There is no equivalent to the NHS in the United States so visits to the doctor can be expensive and hospitalization ruinous. That said, provided you can pay the bills, the health care offered is of a very high standard. Private health insurance is therefore essential and extremely expensive. It is important to check that you are thoroughly covered. If you are travelling back and forth from the UK to a holiday home, insurance can be arranged through your travel agent or through an American insurer as of course it can be if you become a permanent resident. It is said that the average American family spends as much as 15 per cent of its income on health insurance. If you don't have health insurance through an employer, then shop around to find the best and most appropriate insurance agent and policy.

Despite being the smallest state in the Union, Rhode Island has four hundred miles of coastline much favoured by those seeking a relaxed seaside existence.

Public health care does offer Medicare and Medicaid. Medicare primarily caters for people over sixty-five, the disabled and those with certain specified diseases. Medicaid is generally for those on low incomes.

pensions

If you are retired and move to the US permanently, you will be able to receive your UK pension with its annual increments paid directly to your bank account. See www.thepensionservice.gov.uk. If you have not yet retired and move permanently to the USA, your pension will be frozen and the pension you're entitled to will be paid out when you reach the UK age of retirement. Check whether you are eligible to make additional contributions while living abroad so that you eventually receive a full state pension. If you have a personal pension plan, it would be wise to check its terms of payment if you plan to move. The federal government is keen to reduce expenditure on state pensions, so if you become resident and employed in the States, it's advisable to join a company pension plan and even supplement it with a personal pension plan. An independent financial advisor will be able to guide you best.

pets

Since the UK is deemed free from rabies, dogs can be imported to the USA with an Official Certificate of Veterinary Inspection from a government-approved vet (LVI). All dogs are subject to state and local vaccination requirements which you should check before moving. All pet dogs and cats arriving in Hawaii or Guam are subject to quarantine. The US Department of Agriculture has certain restrictions on dogs such as collies or shepherds that are to be used to handle livestock. Some airlines require animals to be accompanied by health certificates so you should contact them well before flying. All cats and dogs are inspected at the port of entry in case they have any diseases that can be transmitted to humans. Visit www.aphis.usda.gov/vs/ncie/pet-info.html for more information and useful links.

The USA is part of the UK Pet Travel Scheme (PETS) so if you plan to return with your pet to the UK you will need to apply for a pet passport. To qualify for one, your pet must be micro-chipped by a UK government-authorized vet (LVI) who will also give it a rabies vaccination and a blood test six months later to check it is protected against the disease. You will need a renewal certificate after each booster injection that must be done between. The pet will also need verification that it has been treated against ticks and tapeworm twenty-four and forty-eight hours before your pet is checked in to travel. When you are travelling, you must make sure that you are using an airline that is an approved carrier and that it is using an approved route under the PETS scheme. Visit the DEFRA website www.defra.gov.uk for all up-to-date information on travelling with your pet.

driving

Americans drive on the right of the road in all states but otherwise each has its own set of rules and regulations. Most of them are the same but you should check what the exceptions are. The speed limit in most states is 65mph (110kmh) except where indicated otherwise. Many states use radar to enforce the speed limits

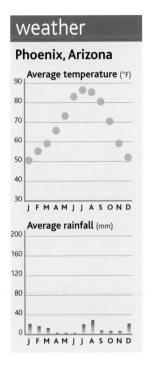

weather

Phoenix, Arizona

Average temperature (°F)

Average rainfall (mm)

The sweeping beaches of New York State's Long Island are overlooked by homesteads typically built on the flats behind the dunes.

strictly, particularly in the Eastern states. Some states allow radar detectors, others do not. The minimum driving age is sixteen in most states though some do not allow unrestricted driving until eighteen.

There is an extensive system of interstate highways and state-maintained roads. Some major motorways are toll roads and called turnpikes. Major interstate highways running north to south have odd numbers from 1–5 on the Pacific Coast to 1–95 on the Atlantic Coast, while those running east to west are evenly numbered, 1–8 near the Mexican border and 1–94 near Canada.

A UK licence is valid for one year.

car

It is not recommended that you import a car to America. It is an expensive and time-consuming affair. Apart from anything, cars can be bought cheaper in the USA. However, if you are determined, you will have to contact the Environmental Protection Agency, the Department of Transportation, the US Customs Service and the Internal Revenue Service. Your car will have to conform to all their regulations and they may have differences of opinion. These websites will help you: www.dot.gov for the Department of Transport's regulations on importing cars; www.nhtsa.dot.gov/cars/rules/import for a list of vehicles previously determined eligible for importation; www.epa.gov/otaq/imports/ or federal regulations concerning vehicle emissions; www.customs.ustreas.gov/xp/cgov/import/ for customs matters.

The good news is that non-residents are allowed to bring their car for up to one year although they will have to post a bond with customs.

taxes

The US tax system is complex and way beyond the scope of this book so you should seek independent financial advice if considering a permanent move. American residents are liable to Federal taxes but each state may impose its own state taxes on top of that; these vary from state to state. They may include additional taxes on income, property, sales, death, gas and cigarettes, 'user fees' for birth certificates, and driving licences. The levels of taxation also differ between states. Some states, including Florida, New Hampshire, Tennessee and Texas, do not have a state income tax. You will need to check what your particular destination demands. If you are moving permanently, good tax planning is essential.

Rental income is taxable but normally, for a non-resident, the double taxation treaty between the US and UK means it will be taxed in the UK. There is capital gains tax (30 per cent of the gain less allowances) to be paid on the sale of the property for non-residents.

House-hunters

Los Angeles

Nicola Wise and Carole Weale
Budget: **£250,000**

Since going on holiday to LA in 1998, Nicola Wise and Carole Weale, have returned a number of times, establishing a wide circle of friends there. They run a training company together in the UK and, if they can sort out green cards, would like eventually to expand their business to the US.

Their search started in the exclusive beach resort of **Malibu**, the American Riviera, renowned for its surfing and celebrity enclave. Only forty minutes from LA airport, this paradise has become a highly sought-after location with house prices rising 17 per cent annually. Nicola and Carole looked at two properties here. The first was a 'condo' or condominium (the American term for an apartment or unit) a twenty-minute drive from Santa Monica. It occupied the end of a small block so was relatively quiet and boasted windows on two sides. The kitchen had been recently remodelled at one end of the compact living/dining area. The master bedroom benefited from high ceilings, lots of hanging space and floor-to-ceiling sliding doors onto a veranda with views to the ocean. It was surprisingly spacious although it needed a little work on the décor. Outside, the large deck provided a great space for entertaining. One point to note was that the land between the property and

Malibu. Two-bedroom condo with open-plan living/dining/ kitchen area, one bathroom; sun deck with ocean views: £235,000.

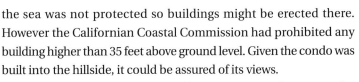

Above: Malibu. Three-bedroom terraced house with two bathrooms, open-plan kitchen-diner, living room; courtyard and shared pool: £245,000.

Above: San Fernando Valley. Three-bedroom ranch-style house with two bathrooms, living room, dining room, kitchen and den; large back garden: £240,000.

Below: San Fernando Valley. Large three-bedroom townhouse with living room, two bathrooms, mezzanine dining area, kitchen; double garage; communal garden and pool: £220,000.

the sea was not protected so buildings might be erected there. However the Californian Coastal Commission had prohibited any building higher than 35 feet above ground level. Given the condo was built into the hillside, it could be assured of its views.

Ten minutes inland, a terraced house in a complex was up for sale. It had a modern American open kitchen-diner and a living room equipped for both summer and winter with central air-conditioning and heating plus a fireplace. The comfortable airy family room used blinds to reduce the heat in the summer and contain it in the winter. The master bedroom was light and spacious and included a sitting area (could be used as a weights area) and a generous walk-in closet. One of the two guest rooms was ideal for conversion into an office. The outside space was green and private with a pool that was heated for eight months in the year. Property is at such a premium that it sells fast and Nicola and Carole had hardly seen it before being told that an offer had been accepted on the house.

However, it was worth being aware that while the property conveyancer was handling the paperwork and checking the buyer had sufficient funds, the seller can accept back-up offers as a security should something go wrong with the first one.

For the next stage of their search, Nicola and Carole moved west to the **San Fernando Valley** between the Santa Monica mountains to the south and the San Gabriele mountains to the north. The nearby Santa Monica National Park provides a welcome escape from the city with plenty of opportunities for hiking, kayaking, walking, bicycling and climbing. There are all sorts of properties available here including ranch houses, condos, town houses, mansions and gated communities. The ranch house they saw had a good-sized living room complete with hardwood floor and wood-burning fireplace. Both the den and the dining room had access to the quarter-acre garden outside. The owners were at pains to reassure Nicola and Carole that they had a building permit for the back extension which they'd used as a dining room. The kitchen had all mod cons and breakfast bar – only the fridge and dishwasher would be leaving. What was used as a child's room would make an ideal office space cum spare room whereas the master bedroom was a good size and benefited from light coming in from windows on two sides. Nicola and Carole thought the property was very well-maintained with lots of space. 'We couldn't fault it.' The garden had been landscaped a year earlier when a patio had been built that was ideal for barbecues but had no pool. However the children's play area could be converted. It would cost around £15,000 for a kidney-shaped pool, including the necessary permit and geological survey.

Only fifteen minutes away was a large townhouse in a condominium complex. Spread over four levels, it offered a living room with tiled floor, electrical and gas fireplace and bar area. The mezzanine dining area was open and light with attractive wooden flooring and a breakfast bar that was ideal for serving cocktails or food. The compact kitchen had a balcony ideal for barbecues. The master bedroom was unusual with high ceilings and mirrors making it look deceptively big. The basement garage space was huge and could be converted into a guest apartment or rented as a garage for somewhere between £400–£500 per month. Outside there was an almost Olympic-sized pool in a peaceful palm-fringed setting with two barbecue areas and a Jacuzzi. Despite all these creature comforts, Nicola and Carole decided to look some more.

Long Beach is about forty minutes' drive from LA airport. In the LA harbour, it combines small-town atmosphere with big-city amenities. It has a vibrant cultural scene with the Long Beach Performing Arts centre playing host to Broadway shows and concerts. With so much on offer, property does not come cheap, but there were a couple of places within Nicola and Carole's price range. The first was an apartment on the twenty-fourth floor of a modern circular tower block. A slick slice of urban living with roomy, tastefully decorated living areas, a kitchen with plenty of storage and built-in appliances, two monster bathrooms and an extra room that was ideal for an office. The current owner had knocked some of the original wall down in the master bedroom that was to be rebuilt before a sale. Getting the work done to their satisfaction should be made a condition of sale. The real selling point was the balcony that encircled the apartment with views over the city on one side and over the harbour on the other. Both Nicola and Carole were very impressed with the property, not forgetting the Olympic-sized pool that came with it. This was an apartment in a prime location that would be easy to rent at about £1,200 per month.

Lastly they travelled to the Long Beach suburbs where they saw a Spanish-style cottage that had been built in 1928. The owners had retained many of the property's original features which gave it oodles of character. The large kitchen overlooked the garden with its picturesque patio awned with trellising. The bright master bedroom had jalousie shutters on the outside. Iron grilles over the windows provided additional security. An authentic Hispanic feature, it meant that the windows could be left open in the summer without worry. The owner had let it be known that he was open to offers, so Nicola and Carole were recommended to make an opening offer of £264,000.

Torn between the last three properties they saw, Nicola and Carole decided that they hadn't found a property that ticked all the boxes. They both loved the space inside the Long Beach apartment and the view beyond, recognizing that this would be the most sensible purchase of the six although they preferred the character of the Spanish cottage and 'wow factor' of the ranch in Malibu. However the search so far had helped them clarify exactly what they wanted and they plan to return to Los Angeles to find their dream place in the sun.

Above: Long Beach. Luxury two-bedroom apartment with two bathrooms, dressing room, kitchen and living room; balcony, communal pool and gym: £260,000.

Below: Long Beach. Three-bedroom Spanish-style cottage with two bathrooms, kitchen, dining room; original features; garden: £275,000.

House-hunters

Florida

Angela and Debbie Hughes
Budget: **£85,000**

St Augustine. Three-bedroom, two-bathroom house with living room and kitchen; on brand new development; double garage: £80,000.

Ormond Beach. Four-bedroom, two-bathroom house with kitchen and dining area, living room, sun room; two patios, terrace, garden; communal pool and tennis courts: £87,000.

Angela Hughes has known her daughter-in-law, Debbie, for eighteen years, since she left school. Debbie was married to Angela's son, Tony, for twelve years. They had all planned to buy a house together until he died from Sudden Adult Death Syndrome. Debbie and Angela felt sure he would have wanted them to continue the search in the part of the world he loved. They planned to share a property, with Angela ultimately retiring to it but spending the winter months there to begin with while Debbie would holiday there. Anticipating the frequent visits of friends and family, they were quite clear about needing three bedrooms and, if possible, a pool.

Florida's First Coast has never been as developed as a big tourist destination but interest has been rising in this historic part of Florida, the first part to be discovered by Europeans in the nineteenth century. Property prices have always tended to be lower here than in the rest of Florida, being further from Orlando and Miami, but prices are on the rise.

They started their search in **St Augustine**, the oldest town in the USA. Founded in 1565, St Augustine is full of beautiful historic buildings including the impressive Flager College and the Bridge of Lions. The most unusual building is the Castillo de San Marcos built from *coquilla*, a locally quarried rock made of compressed seashells. The place is popular with North American retirees although few foreigners have as yet bought there. Angela and Debbie visited a show home on a new development just outside town. The entrance led into a wide entry hall that had the dining area to the right and a sitting area on the left. The large open kitchen offered lots of cupboard space, a low divide separating it from the formal living room – ideal for being able to socialize while cooking. The master bedroom was big enough for a party as was the en suite bathroom. Outside the plot had enough room for a pool although they would need planning permission. Unlikely to be difficult to get, it would take between four and six weeks to get, but the headache of the necessary paperwork could be removed by handing over to a pool contractor who would do that side of the work for about £100. Ultimately Debbie and Angela felt it was too remote and too quiet for them.

They continued their search in the exclusive resort of **Ormond Beach**, made famous by hosting the first motor races in 1903. Today racing enthusiasts flock here for vintage car parades and annual historical re-enactments of the original races. It was also the home of the wealthy tycoon, John D. Rockefeller who claimed this part of Florida was the cleanest and healthiest part of the world. Outside the town proper are some leafy residential areas and it was here that Debbie and Angela saw a timber and brick cottage in a gated community. Inside the floors were tiled throughout and the large kitchen fitted with unique green units and all mod cons. Although there was plenty of room in the kitchen for a table, there was also a formal dining area. The living area had a working fireplace and alcove shelving. There were two bedrooms on the ground floor, one the en suite master bathroom and, up the unusual central staircase, there were two more, one of which was currently used as a TV room. It struck Debbie and Angela as a very peaceful area with a family feel to the estate. They also liked the fact that all the houses were architecturally different. The fact that it was a gated community ensured privacy, security and quiet as there was no through traffic. They would have to take into account that there was a £380 annual fee for the maintenance of the estate. Angela loved it but Debbie was concerned that the garden was in constant shade.

St Augustine Beach. Two-bedroom, two-bathroom ground-floor apartment with open-plan kitchen-diner, living room and veranda; situated on golf course with communal pool and residents' bar: £83,000.

Next, they travelled towards **St Augustine Beach** which lies between the Atlantic and the Intracoastal Waterway. Today used for cruises and fishing, the Waterway is a 1,500-mile canal route from Boston to Southern Florida. Built in the mid-twentieth century, it proved useful during the Second World War when it provided a protected trading route out of sight and reach of German U-boats. There are some magnificent properties overlooking beach and waterway, some with private jetties and moorings. These can sell for up to £3,000,000 but nearby there was a stylish apartment for sale that fell within Debbie and Angela's budget. The roomy living room was deceptively light thanks to the mirrors lining one wall and gave onto a veranda with views over the fairway and lake. The comfortable kitchen featured a double American fridge and a small breakfast table near the window. The winning feature of the master bedroom was the enclosed veranda, making it possible to sleep with the french windows open at night. This really captured the two women's imagination as they saw themselves sitting there, enjoying a morning coffee. Overall they loved the design of the property, the high ceilings, space and views. The complex had a lot to offer, even an on-site recreation club that for a membership fee of £20 included yoga and exercise classes and two social evenings a month. However, on reflection, they decided despite the views, the place didn't have the character they were looking for.

Palm Coast. Floridian style bungalow with three bedrooms, two bathrooms, kitchen, dining room and living room; additional summer kitchen; pool, Jacuzzi, outside seating area and double garage: £144,000.

They finished their search in **Palm Coast**, a Floridian new town developed twenty-five years ago by a New York building firm. They bought up 68,000 acres of land, laid 500 miles of roads and built 2,000 houses a year. To encourage the development of the community they offered free land to schools and places of worship. Palm Coast has

the second lowest tax rate in Florida and properties are snapped up by US holidaymakers and retirees. The house Angela and Debbie visited was over their budget but offered everything they wanted including a fabulous pool. The large formal living/dining area was light and white with ceiling fans and nooks and crannies in the walls lending it character. The kitchen, white units with green walls and worktop trim had almost more cupboards than you could count. The family room had plenty of room for an outsize TV screen but Debbie was impressed by the use that had been made of the available light with sloping ceilings, double windows and a mirror over the fireplace. They were both bowled over by the generous master bedroom and en suite bathroom but the clinching factor was the pool and attractive surrounding area complete with small kitchen area. As far as Debbie and Angela were concerned, the property was well thought out with each room being light and brighter than the last. For them, it was the perfect Floridian home with its bright exterior colours, big windows and outside summer kitchen. Once the show house of the estate, it had all the extra features including the high cathedral ceilings, executive bath and bug frame over the pool. The latter made the pool easy to keep clean with the addition of chlorine tablets every week, or in absentia, there was always the pool boy who would do it for £15 per month.

The last property was the one that captured their imaginations. However they needed more time to sort out their finances before being able to commit to it. Having returned to the UK, they planned to return to Florida to continue their search in the sun.

House-hunters

Virginia
Janice and Gordon Ballard
Budget: £120,000

Retirement has brought Gordon and Janice Ballard the opportunity to travel and they are keen to establish an American base for themselves. Gordon worked for an investment bank in the City before retiring eight years ago and was looking forward to taking up painting. Janice ran her own recruitment and training business until she retired recently. Having worked all their lives, they wanted somewhere warm where they could spend the winter months. They both loved the diversity of America, whether the different landscapes, the people or its history. They wanted to find what they regarded as a typical American house – big, comfortable and modern. An important consideration was lack of maintenance. The Ballards needed to be able to pack up and go without worrying about the upkeep of their home. Otherwise, they were open-minded.

Their search began in **Hampton** on a long peninsula where the Chesapeake Bay sweeps out to the Atlantic Ocean. A thriving seaside city, it has won an award as an 'All-America City' for its high standard of living. It is home to the NASA Langley Research Centre where America's first astronauts trained, and to the futuristically shaped Coliseum concert hall, a major venue for sports and music events. Its history is reflected in the colonial style of many of its buildings. The property market around Hampton was very strong, the average cost of a three-bed family home in the suburbs being £98,000. The Ballards were warned that properties tended to move very quickly with sellers often receiving offers within hours of their property going on the market.

Above: Hampton. Two-bedroom condo with living room, kitchen/diner, bathroom and balcony; shared pool: £66,000.

The first house they saw there was a top-floor two-bed condo with plenty of original features in a condominium. Bookshelves flanked the fireplace in the light elegant living room with picture windows overlooking Pine Cone Harbour. A dream kitchen had tiled floor, masses of cupboards, an island with breakfast bar and all appliances. A good-size master bedroom with attractive arched window was complemented by the sea green en suite bathroom with huge shower cubicle. Outside, use of the inviting pool came with acquisition of the property. Down at the marina, there was an entertainment deck and club house that would make meeting people easy, particularly during the happy hour that happened every evening at 5 pm. The clubhouse could also be hired for £30 a day for parties. Both the Ballards agreed that they couldn't waste the possibility of acquiring a mooring and taking up a boating life. The moorings were £40 to rent or £1,800–£3,000 to buy, depending on the depth of the water.

The next property they saw was very different. Recently restored and in the heart of the community of **Newport News**, it was just a two-minute drive from the James River. A pretty weatherboard house had all the original wooden floors restored. The living room had a big fireplace and windows on three sides. Light flooded through the one large window in the formal dining room. There was good use of space in the kitchen with lots of cupboards, a smart black-and-white tiled floor and all appliances included. The master bedroom was simple and tastefully decorated in soft colours with pine timber flooring and a large wardrobe. A sizable decking area led to a designed garden with genuine old brick paths. The house was in remarkable condition and the current owners had done a fabulous job of restoration. As the house was in a preservation area, the owners had to apply to the review board if they wanted to make any exterior changes. There were strict regulations on the materials and colours to be used. When they

Below: Hampton. Three-bedroom house with two living rooms, two bathrooms, study; large back garden and secluded deck: £117,000.

Below: Virginia's Eastern Shore. Three storey arts-and-crafts house with two living rooms, dining room, kitchen, bathroom, converted loft and basement; two acres land; separate garage and workshop: £123,000.

were asked what they thought about cutting down one of the gum trees growing near the back of the house, Janice replied, 'It's too beautiful a house to worry about a tree.'

Virginia's Eastern Shore is a 70-mile long peninsula lying across the Chesapeake Bay. There's a relaxed pace of life in the peninsula's sleepy towns and picturesque countryside where the economy relies on fishing and agriculture. Many of the buildings date back to the 1800s, and are a mix of colonial revival, neo-classic and Victorian. The property market is slower than on mainland Virginia, an average house costing around £77,000. This is the last undeveloped bit of the Atlantic shoreline and residents are anxious to keep it that way. The first house Gordon and Janice saw was a traditional arts and crafts house built in the late 1800s. With plenty of kerb appeal, this house had the traditional porches running round three-quarters of the house, both screened and open. The Ballards loved the grandeur of the living room with its old English brick fireplace, sash windows and original features. The dining room was at the back of the house and had a beautiful bay window. The tiled kitchen had original tongue-and-groove pine walls and pine units. Upstairs the bedrooms were of a good size although Janice thought she might redecorate the bathrooms. Surrounding it, were two acres of land on which was a three-car garage. Ultimately they decided it was too far away from civilization for them

Next up was something very different. A trailer home located in **Chesapeake Bay** just a stone's throw from the water's edge and part of a quiet community. It had been brought to the site in 2002 and had the merit of being moveable should Gordon and Janice find another area of land to lease. Much bigger inside than expected, the rooms were light, one leading to another, with some excellent views of the bay. At one end of the house was a wheelchair ramp that could be dismantled and replaced with a deck at a cost of around £2,500. Despite the attractions of the setting, the Ballards knew immediately it was not for them.

They continued their search in **Chincoteague**, a seasonal beach resort and wildlife preserve five miles from the mainland. The island is world-famous for its oyster beds and clam shoals, otherwise it offers plenty of opportunities for water sports on its varied coast of wetlands and beaches. Property prices here are high by Virginian standards and houses that come on the market are usually snapped up quickly. The first property the Ballards saw was a compact cottage in the heart of the main town of Chincoteague, within easy reach of shops, restaurants and the beach. They felt that

Below: Chincoteague. Two-bedroom cottage with living room, kitchen/diner, bathroom; garden, deck: £110,000.

the living room could do with another window and needed some personality stamping on it, probably with colour. That set the tone of the visit as they saw the dark wood kitchen, the compact bathroom and the rather joyless master bedroom. There was plenty of parking space for a car and boat. If the Ballards wanted to extend the house to add another bathroom, it would cost £60 per square metre, and therefore £1,800 for a twenty-by-ten-square-foot extension. Janice thought the interior was too dark and smelly and was put off by the neighbour's dog penned up close by.

Lastly they returned to the mainland where they viewed a house that had been built on stilts on the beach. Not surprisingly, the views from every room were second to none. Overall the interior of the property was a bit dated, particularly the dark wood kitchen. A pleasant open-plan living area had a breakfast table and painted white chairs. The long living room benefited from a galleried landing under the high ceiling. Gordon and Janice thought the addition of plate-glass sliding doors would take full advantage of the view and from the addition of skylights in the ceiling, giving light to the room below and views from the landing. Three two-by-four-foot windows, at a cost of £350 each, would be well worth the expense. The master bedroom was double-glazed for soundproofing with screens to deter any bugs. The en suite bathroom needed a facelift. The setting was magical with one hundred feet of private beachfront; however, Gordon and Janice were put off by the thought of mosquitoes.

Having seen six properties, they were torn between the two Hampton properties. The only course of action was to revisit them both. Having done that, the Ballards made enquiries about buying the condo, only to find the owner had taken it off the market. Undeterred, the Ballards plan to return to Hampton to view more properties with the hope of finding the ideal base for their American travels.

Above: Virginia's Eastern Shore. Large three-bedroom beach house with two bathrooms, kitchen/diner, enclosed deck; all furniture included; one acre land: £139,000.

Ex-pat experience

Gulf Coast, Florida

Sylvia and Derek Bird

Flying home from Florida on Christmas Day seven or eight years ago, florist Sylvia Bird asked herself what on earth she was doing. She had been working there for the previous month and was rushing home to

be with her husband Derek, who works as ground staff with one of the major airlines, and their two grown sons. They decided to spend the next Christmas in Florida on a family holiday. They rented an apartment in Sanibel Harbour Resort, overlooking the dolphins and ospreys in San Carlos Bay. It was when her sister talked about buying an apartment in the same block that Derek and Sylvia suggested they should all buy a home together.

Sylvia stayed on for another week, hunting for something with four bedrooms, three bathrooms and a pool that would suit them all. Having hired a car, she drove around looking at various 'subdivisions' or building developments. 'I found a site I liked where building had only just started. There was no one there but I returned on the morning I was leaving, arriving at the same time as the agent who showed me the plans then emailed me all the necessary information. Two months later we returned to see the show home, loved it and picked our site. Because we'd got in so early, we had the pick of the site, choosing a private south-facing spot that overlooks the lake for which we put down a $200 deposit.' For less than £200,000, the Birds went on to build their dream home that met all their specifications. They had sold a property in the UK so were cash buyers, making the financial transactions simple. The building company supplied a solicitor and recommended an independent one. Cautious, Sylvia took the contract to a solicitor in the UK but he simply approved it. The house was built in six months along with the other fifty or so properties on the site, and at that point the Birds paid the balance of the purchase price.

Since then the family have been as often as they can. The zoning regulations prohibit them from renting. 'I see it as a home not a holiday home, so that's fine by us,' says Sylvia. There are other restrictions such as a ban on hanging out washing, on parking a boat or commercial vehicle, on putting up fencing. 'One neighbour thought he was doing everyone a favour by fencing his dogs in, but everyone preferred the dogs loose and no fencing, so it was taken down.'

The most recent time they were there, she found hiring a car for six weeks was too expensive so made the decision to buy one. What she wasn't expecting was a driving test. But before she could have a number plate, she had to have insurance and to get insurance she was told she would have to pay $1,400 for six months. The alternative was to take a theory test on screen consisting of forty questions on the Highway Code plus a driving test in her new car. Having passed them both, she handed over $20 for her US licence.

The Birds have been lucky in that their neighbours have been 'wonderful' and number Americans from Ohio, New York and Boston. They have superb facilities including a sports arena, ice rink, cinemas, shops and restaurants on their doorstep. They are over-run with golfing communities, although Sylvia has yet to become addicted to the game, and only a fifteen-minute drive from Fort Myers Beach, one of the beautiful beaches on the Gulf of Mexico. 'It's not as cosmopolitan as Miami nor as busy as Fort Lauderdale,' observes Sylvia. 'It's more like Palm Beach here.' They are residents in Lee County (named after Gen. Robert E. Lee) where the local museums are the Thomas Edison and Henry Ford Winter Estates. Apparently both families used to winter in Florida. Derek plans to retire in 2005 and knows exactly where he wants to live. Sylvia has qualified and is an accredited member of the American Institute of Floral Designers. She has also progressed within the association and is currently a Director at Large on the Board as well as President Elect of the North East Region of AIFD. She hopes to be able to get a green card and be able to continue working in Florida.

'I recently did the flowers for our neighbour's daughter's wedding in Sanibel. I was encouraged that the hotel liked them and feel confident that, with a green card, I could set up a business here.' Buying their new home marks the start of a whole new life for them both.

'One neighbour thought he was doing everyone a favour by fencing his dogs in, but everyone preferred the dogs loose and no fencing, so it was taken down.'

South Africa

Introduction

A twelve-hour flight from Britain, South Africa is only two hours ahead of UK time in the British winter (one hour in summer), so there's no jetlag, making it an ideal place for short breaks. With year-round sunshine and miles of white sandy beaches, this area is fast becoming an alternative destination to the Caribbean. South Africa is vast: fifth largest country by population in Africa and the combined size of Germany, France, Italy, Belgium and the Netherlands. It is bordered by Namibia, Botswana, Zimbabwe, Mozambique and Swaziland, with its 3,000 kilometre coastline washed by the Atlantic Ocean to the west, and the warm currents of the Indian Ocean to the east, both with scenic coastlines and sweeping beaches. Within the country there is wide geographical diversity with landscapes that range from snow-capped mountains, dense forests, semi-deserts, savannah and grassland to man-made environments such as twenty-first-century cityscapes, vineyards and a multitude of golf courses. The country boasts a solid infrastructure with good air links and a first-class road system.

With a climate that varies from Mediterranean in the Cape to subtropical in KwaZulu-Natal, the emphasis is very much on the outdoor life. Whether bungee-jumping, surfing, trekking, white-water rafting or swimming with great white sharks, there's something to suit every adrenalin junkie. Otherwise the vibrant cities are alive with the best in restaurants, cafés, nightclubs, theatres and cinemas. Outside them lie numerous world-class wineries, superb opportunities for whale-watching, bird-watching, fishing, plenty of game reserves where animals roam wild, international standard golf courses and, of course, spectacular scenery that may be enjoyed by car, on horseback or on foot. Throughout the country lie quiet towns and villages retaining their traditional architecture and values. Local cuisine throughout South Africa offers a rich and plentiful variety of fish and meat. Favourite dishes include the Malay *bobotie* (baked mince with apricot, almond, chutney and curry spices), *boerewors* (beef and pork sausages), *sosaties* (marinated pork or lamb kebabs) and *bredie* (meat or fish stew with vegetables and chillies). It is not just the Afrikaners who enjoy their *potjies* (succulent stews) and *braaivleis* or barbecued meat, usually eaten outdoors at the ubiquitous *braai* which is very much part of the South African culture. Fruit and vegetables are grown throughout the Western Cape while Natal is known for its sugar cane.

This is the rainbow nation where, following the collapse of apartheid, work goes on to build a multi-ethnic culture with economic stability. By far the majority of the South African population is composed of black Africans, proud of their ethnic roots. Ten per cent of the population is white of whom the majority is Afrikaners of Dutch origin, but a sizeable chunk is of British descent and speak English as a first language. English is also the language of commerce. The largest ethnic groups are Xhosa, Zulu, Sotho and Tswana. Eleven official languages are spoken: Afrikaans (72 per cent of Afrikaans speakers belong to the Coloured community of mixed

Previous page: Boschendal Manor House sits at the gateway to the Franschhoek Valley in the heart of South Africa's wine region.

facts

Capital: Pretoria

Area: 1,219,912 sq km

Highest point: Njesuthi (3,408 m)

Lowest point: Atlantic (0 m)

Coastline: 2,798 km

Population: 43,768,678

Currency: and (ZAR)

Time zone: GMT + 2 hours

Electricity: 220V at 50Hz

Weights and measures: Metric

Religions: Christian, Muslim, Hindu

Languages: Afrikaans, English, Ndebele, Pedi, Sotho, Swazi, Tsonga, Tswana, Venda, Xhosa, Zulu

Government: Republic

International dialling code: 00 27

National holiday: 27 April, Freedom Day

Cape Malay, Khoi and San origins), English, Ndebele, Pedi, Sotho, Tswana, siSwati, Venda and Tsonga, Xhosa, Zulu. However English is understood pretty much everywhere. This is a country where there are plenty of reminders of its turbulent past yet there is no doubt that it is resolutely looking towards the future.

This section will focus largely on the coastal belt of South Africa where the majority of British people looking for a new home and a new life are understandably drawn.

The first white settlers arrived in South Africa in the mid-seventeenth century. In 1652, a Dutchman, Jan van Riebeeck, landed at Table Bay with a hundred men and set about building a fort. As the colony expanded, French Huguenots added to their number. In 1795, the British became the occupying power although their position was precarious until 1814 when they finally established themselves more firmly. At about the same time, the Zulus emerged as a powerful force that was to conflict with both the Boers (literally 'farmers') and the British until Zululand was annexed to become part of Natal. In the 1830s, a group of Afrikaner pioneers, the Voortrekkers, disgusted by the British abolition of slavery in 1834, struck out for the interior. This was the Great Trek that led to the establishment of the Boer republics of the Orange Free State and the Transvaal.

An uneasy peace existed between the British and the Boers that was eventually blown apart by the discovery of diamonds in Kimberley in the 1860s and, later, of gold on the Witwaterstrand, the site of Johannesberg. The Anglo-Boer War raged for three years until the Boers conceded defeat in 1902. In 1910, Transvaal, Orange Free State, Cape and Natal became the Union of South Africa. Blacks were excluded from the arrangement so the South African Native National Congress was formed, later to become the ANC, in order to establish their recognition by the white society. In 1948, the National Party was elected by the white electorate. Throughout the 1950s, they worked to implement their apartheid policies. For the following fifty years the struggle to establish black people's rights shaped country until, in 1994, the ANC won the national election and Nelson Mandela set the country on the road to democracy.

the cape peninsula

Affectionately known as the 'mother city', **Cape Town** is South Africa's number one tourist spot. Sandstone mountains encircle the city, forming a bowl in which the main city of Cape Town sits, facing out to the Atlantic Ocean. Table Mountain is the most famous of these summits, and is a symbol of the city the world over. The city was established by the Dutch in 1652 as a supply depot for ships heading to the Far East. The British Empire took possession in 1806 and its legacy can still be felt today. Magnificent colonial buildings stand proud with leafy Victorian suburbs, with the distinctive bright colours of the historic Malay quarter of Bo-Kaap and with the best in modern residential and commercial architecture.

The oldest port in the whole country, Cape Town is still an important trading area, attracting native Africans who sell their carpets, jewellery and statues in the daily markets. Contrasting with those is the bustle of the modern developments on the Victoria and Alfred Waterfront, once a working harbour, now a fashionable shopping and entertainment area, and the Century city shopping and leisure complex on the outskirts of town. Cape Town also boasts City Gardens, one of the most beautiful urban parks in the country, flanked by the Houses of Parliament, museums and galleries and not far from the Castle of Good Hope. The seventeenth-century castle was built to defend the early Dutch colony, later becoming the centre of all administrative, social and military activities in the colony.

The buzz of this thoroughly cosmopolitan city is only minutes away from stunning countryside and idyllic beaches. The affluent suburbs of **Clifton**, **Sandy Bay** and **Camps Bay** offer sensational ocean views. There are great beaches here but the sea can be cold, far colder than across the peninsula at **False Bay** where a number of quiet settlements stretch between **Muizenburg** and **Simonstown**, the most attractive of them all. One of the most upmarket inland suburbs is **Constantia**, named by Governor Simon van der Stel who settled there in 1685 and established the first wine-making region in South Africa. South of the city lies the scenic Cape of Good Hope Nature Reserve founded in 1939. Cape Town offers the very best in urban living with all manner of outdoor activities available right on its doorstep.

See www.capetourism.org for more tourist information.

weather

Cape Town

Average temperature (°F)

Average rainfall (mm)

the western cape

The Western Cape offers a little bit of everything South African from breathtaking scenery, native forests, endless unspoilt beaches, areas of semi-desert and the best whale-watching in the world. It is thought that the Portuguese explorer Vasco de Gama was the first European to land in the region at the mouth of Berg River in 1497.

North of Cape Town, the Atlantic shoreline offers more great beaches and a number of resort towns, most of them boasting first-class seafood restaurants. Over the last fifteen years, the area has developed with the result that many coastal properties are at a premium. **Bloubergstrand** has a fabled view of Table Mountain and in recent years has become a desirable residential area. Once a small fishing village, **Langebaan** has been heavily developed and with **Saldanha**, **Port Owen**, **Dwarskerbos**, **Lambert's Bay** and other coastal resorts offers splendid opportunities for watersports and fishing. The wetlands of the Langebaan Lagoon and the West Coast National Park make it a haven for birdwatchers and animal

Clifton is regarded as Cape Town's most glamorous beach overlooked by correspondingly desirable properties.

lovers. The little town of **Velddrif** is synonymous with *bokkems*, dried fish eaten with white wine or bread, apricot jam and coffee.

Inland, **Darling** is a busy agricultural town surrounded by arable, cattle and sheep farming, and vineyards. The whole area is renowned for the splendour of its spring (July to September) wild flowers most particularly in the far north in the wild plains of Namaqualand. Every year, Darling hosts a spring flower festival. The mountain valleys are spotted with sleepy farming towns and villages. The Breede River Valley in particular is known for its fruit farms, wineries and as South Africa's leading racehorse breeding area. The picture-book villages are popular as getaways from Cape Town: the olde-worlde charm of **Greyton**'s oak-lined streets; the preserved nineteenth-century thatched architecture of **McGregor**; the hot springs and stunning views of **Rawsonville**; the post-earthquake perfectly restored eighteenth- and nineteenth-century buildings of **Tulbagh**.

A forty-five-minute drive east from Cape Town lies one of the most visited areas of South Africa. The **Winelands** were discovered in 1687 by Simon van der Stel. Gradually a settlement of farmers came to this fertile area on the Eerste River and the town of **Stellenbosch** was declared in 1685. As the area prospered so other towns were founded, most notably **Paarl** and **Franschoek**. Today, with its oak-lined streets and restored Cape Dutch, Victorian and Georgian houses, Stellenbosch is at the heart of a thriving wine-producing region. The prevailing winds make the temperature slightly cooler and the air more humid in this area – perfect for growing grapes. Over 150 different estates in the Winelands produce both red and white wines. With over a dozen wine routes, some of the best restaurants in the whole country, unforgettable walking trails, the area's popularity is not surprising. Cape Dutch homesteads are scattered through the valleys, on the foothills of mountain ranges and among the vineyards and orchards.

Travelling east brings one to the **Overberg** where there are some pleasant inland villages and unique scenery given up to nature reserves, vineyards, mountains and farmland. However, the big draw of the area is the Whale Coast, still relatively underdeveloped. Billed in tourist information as the 'best-kept secret of South Africa' it is cut off from the rest of South Africa by the Riviersonderend, Langeberg and Outeniqua mountain ranges. In 1828 the construction of Lowry's Pass enabled the early settlers to get a toehold in it. It boasts the southernmost tip of the continent, Cape Agulhas, dividing the Atlantic from the Indian Ocean. The foothills of the mountains merge with rolling farmlands.

On the coast is a string of modest resort towns, the exception being **Hermanus** which has profited as one of the best land-based whale-watching sites in the world and is spectacularly sited at the foot of mountains. A horn-blowing towncrier directs watchers to the best viewing points. Some of the best beaches in the Cape are on hand – long white dune-backed swathes of sand. The towns of the Overberg are small and compact with great rural charm. **Arniston** with its 200-year-old thatched, white-washed cottages; **Stanford** with its unprepossessing Victorian architecture; the white-washed cottages of **Elim**, known for its thatchers, vineyards

weather

Durban

Average temperature (°F)

Average rainfall (mm)

and fynbos, focus on the Moravian Church; **Kleinmond** lies on a lagoon and is a favourite holiday destination; **Swellendam** was founded in 1746 at the foot of the Langeberg mountains and is famous for its well-preserved historic architecture, its youngberries and dairy and wheat farming. Stuck between the Winelands and the Garden Route, Overberg is often overlooked but has plenty of attractions of its own – golf, hiking, birdwatching, canoeing, mountain biking, architecture, history, fynbos and flower trails.

The western coast is most famous for its **Garden Route** where, over the past two years there has been a huge increase in the number of British people buying property. It's hard to resist the allure of this narrow strip of land that runs from Mossel Bay to Storms River Mouth and is considered by many to be paradise on earth. Rivers rush through the heavily forested landscape towards the much-lauded coastline. Busy resorts vie for attention with the neighbouring wilderness. Between the principal coastal towns of Mossel Bay, Knysna and Plettenberg (familiarly known as 'Plett') lie other smaller but equally appealing resort towns and villages.

Mossel Bay has a considerable industrial area and is heavily developed for tourists. Its must-sees are the Bartholomeu Dias Museum Complex, named after the explorer, and Seal Island, home to colonies of African penguins and Cape fur seals. Its year-round mild climate gained it entry into the *Guinness Book of Records*. More sophisticated is **Knysna**, situated on a lagoon and protected by hills of pine and gum plantations. Once a dozy hippy hideaway, Knysna has skipped into the twenty-first century while retaining its historic centre of wide leafy streets and Victorian houses. The only thing it lacks is a beach but it's not far to **Buffalo Bay**, **Wilderness** or **Noetzie**. What it does have is its forests, once home to the Khoikoi clans and the elephant, now verging on extinction.

Plettenberg Bay is a playground of the rich, perched on sandstone cliffs affording fantastic ocean views to most of its residents. The resort is characterized by its lagoons, rocky peninsular, sweeping beaches and nearby nature reserves. In 1630, the Portuguese survivors of a shipwreck in the bay named it *Baia Formosa* – 'Beautiful Bay'.

See www.capetourism.org for more tourist information.

the eastern cape

The Eastern Cape is far less visited than its neighbour although it has many similar attractions. The landscape is as dramatic and varied as anywhere along the east coast. Part of the Tsitsikamma National Park spreads into the region from Western Cape. The provincial capital is **Port Elizabeth**, a sprawling industrial city where shanty towns exist beside affluent suburbs. The surrounding region is particularly known as the bedrock for South Africa's black trade unions out of which emerged both Nelson Mandela and Steve Biko. The nearest major attraction is the Addo Elephant Park. Along the coast lie small resort towns that barely function outside the holiday seasons. Among them is **Jeffreys Bay** that springs to life when the surfers hit town looking for the perfect wave. On a long dune-backed bay, the

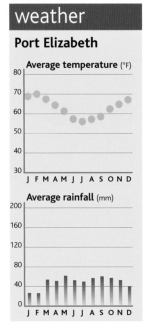

weather

Port Elizabeth

Average temperature (°F)

80
70
60
50
40
30

J F M A M J J A S O N D

Average rainfall (mm)

200
160
120
80
40
0

J F M A M J J A S O N D

picturesque thatched white-walled homes of **St Francis Bay** line a network of canals. Nearby is **Oyster Bay**, with long stretches of sandy beach and unspoiled nature. **Kenton-on-Sea** is a small beautifully situated resort, between the mouths of the Boesmans and the Kariega Rivers. Deserted white-sanded beaches stretch up the coast, buffeted by the afternoon winter winds.

The man-made islands and canals of Port Alfred make it an extremely desirable destination for holiday-home owners.

Just inland, lies **Grahamstown**, host to a National Arts Festival every year. Known for its fifty churches, university and top schools, it also retains many restored historic buildings and is within easy reach of various private game reserves, the Baviaanskloof Wilderness Area and the picture-perfect provincial towns of **Graaff-Reinet** and **Nieu Bethesda**. Founded in 1786, Graaff-Reinet is the oldest town in the area with a fair share of listed buildings while the peaceful Nieu Bethesda is known for The Owl House home, the showcase for the artist Helen Martins. Both are close to the Karoo Nature Reserve where you'll find the imposing Valley of Desolation. North of **East London** lies the Wild Coast. Once the Transkrei homeland, disenfranchised during apartheid, it is home to the Xhosa. Very few white people have settled there. However the coastline is spectacular and unspoilt with charming small communities such as **Coffee Bay** and **Port St Johns**. Its plus points are tropical vegetation, dramatic cliffs and great beaches and some beautiful natural rock formations such as Hole-in-the-Wall near Coffee Bay.

See www.sa-eastcape.co.za for more tourist information.

kwazulu-natal

On Christmas Day, 1497, the Portuguese navigator, Vasco da Gama, sighted these forested shores and named them Rio de Natal or Christmas River. The original settlement has developed over the centuries into the city of **Durban**, a vibrant cultural melting pot. The British gained a toehold in 1824 when they established the settlement of Port Natal. Threatened over the years by the Boers and the Zulus, they finally annexed the Colony of Natal in 1843 and the number of immigrants subsequently rose. Today the city presents an intriguing fusion of European, Indian and Zulu influences. The historical centre of the city boasts some attractively restored buildings and major museums. To the west lies the busy Indian district complete with union-style architecture interrupted by minarets and steeples. The Golden Mile adequately sums up the six-kilometre Durban seafront, popular with swimmers, surfers and visitors to the Sea World and Water World amusement parks. The city is completely geared up to tourism with all the pleasures afforded by the Indian Ocean overlooked by high-rise hotels and apartments. But Durban has more than just beaches and harbours. It also sports a number of theatres, art galleries, shopping centres, museums, and a lively nightlife. The most sought-after residential district is the Berea, built high on a ridge west of the centre of town. One of Durban's oldest suburbs, it enjoys spectacular views of the Ocean and has the Botanic Gardens offering a shady alternative.

Outside the city, the beaches to the north and south are quieter than the city beach and are a holiday magnet for families from Johannesburg and its surrounds.

The Hibiscus Coast, just an hour and a half south of Durban is all about the outdoor life. It extends from **Hibberdene** to **Port Edward** with its neighbouring Wild Coast Sun, a casino resort, and the Mtamvuna Nature Reserve. Between them are strung numerous lively resorts, among them **Uvongo** where a twenty-three-metre waterfall plunges into a lagoon. **Port Shepstone** is the commercial centre of the sugar cane and sub-tropical fruit farming community. **Margate** and **Ramsgate** almost blur into one another but Ramsgate is distinguished from its brasher sister town by a certain lazy old-fashioned charm. With just about all the facilities holidaymakers could want, the beaches here are the most popular on the East Coast of South Africa but there are plenty of more secluded beaches too. This coast is also known as the Golf Coast thanks to its eleven championship golf courses, with green fees costing as little as £7. Thanks to its year-round temperate climate (but extremely humid and hot in summer), this is one of Africa's greenest regions and a warmer winter alternative to the beaches further south. Other drawcards here include the Oribi Gorge Nature Reserve and the dive site at Aliwal Shoal.

North of Durban lies the **Dolphin Coast**, known for its visiting bottle-nosed dolphins. Less developed than the south coast, it boasts a number of quieter, attractive resorts. **Umhlanga Rocks** is the closest resort to Durban with reputedly the biggest shopping mall in the southern hemisphere. Other attractions are its three-kilometre promenade above the wide beaches and the areas of wetland and forest that lie to the north. **Ballito**, though only originated in 1953, is now considered the pearl of the coast. It boasts more fabulous beaches lined with holiday apartments and hotels and provides a high entertainment quota. Ballito is becoming more and more popular as a holiday destination, as are **Salt Rock** and **Shaka's Rock**. Getting away from the coast there are numerous nature reserves and some first-class golf courses. Inland rural towns laze among the sugar cane plantations. Evidence of Zulu history abounds. Much further inland, in the hilly thornveld of Central Zululand, are the legendary battlefield sites where the Zulus first fought the Boers then the British, and where the British then fought the Boers.

North-west of Durban, through the scenic Valley of a Thousand Hills dotted with Zulu homesteads, lies **Pietermaritzburg**. The city was founded in 1838 by the Voortrekkers following their defeat of the Zulus at Blood River. Now the provincial capital of the region, its heritage is obvious in the perfectly preserved Victorian architecture which today is juxtaposed with more modern design. The city centre and western suburbs contain museums, historic buildings, galleries and monuments to its past. From Pietermaritzburg, it's only a short way to the foothills of the Drakensburg Mountains, known as the **Midlands**. Here the climate is pleasant throughout the year, the landscape is green and hilly, predominantly pasture and forests. The legacy of the British is evident in the number of country clubs, tea shops, smart boarding schools and trout-fishing and polo clubs. The scenery and outdoor activities on offer are the draws over the towns in the area which are unremarkable.

See www.kzn.org.za for more tourist information.

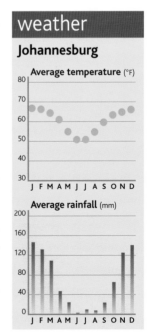

weather

Johannesburg

Average temperature (°F)

J F M A M J J A S O N D

Average rainfall (mm)

J F M A M J J A S O N D

gauteng

A tiny region, Gauteng is the economic heartland of South Africa. It is unlikely that anyone in search of a holiday home would come here but it is impossible to ignore its two major cities, Johannesburg and Pretoria. **Jo'burg** is a tough and racy cosmopolitan city with a reputation for trouble. Gold was discovered here in 1886 and despite having become the largest and richest city in the country, it is neither the political nor economic capital. Here the divisions of old apartheid can still be seen in the contrast between the affluent, security-bound housing for white people in the suburbs and the extensive shanty towns housing the impoverished black people. There are huge pressures on housing and law and order here. The original city centre now lies virtually derelict while a new business quarter has been built in the north close to the smart residential suburbs. Of those, the best known are Sandton and Randberg, both with thriving café culture and sophisticated retail opportunities. **Pretoria**, the administrative capital, is an elegant city to the south-west of Jo'burg where the streets are lined with brightly flowering jacaranda trees. Way back in the nineteenth century, men were drawn to the area by the prospect of wealth from the gold mines; now they come to the biggest attraction of all, the **Kruger National Park**, almost as big as Wales, home to the big five – lion, leopard, rhino, buffalo and elephant – and plenty more.

The streets of modern Pretoria are graced with historic and modern architecture, landscaped parks and jacaranda trees.

See www.gauteng.net for more tourist information.

The property market

The end of apartheid, closely followed by South Africa's entry into the global economy in 1994, paved the way for ever-increasing numbers of foreigners heading for this vast country to buy property. Attracted here for several reasons, not least the relatively cheap price of real estate, low cost of living, glorious scenery and attractive climate, they come looking for a holiday home, or a primary residence to serve as a base for a new life and career, or somewhere to retire.

Demand has been fuelled by aggressive marketing by the country's leading estate agents, many of whom have either offices or representation in the UK. Recent statistics from one company show that a quarter of residential property buyers in the Cape Town area are foreigners, of whom over half are British. Following in their wake are Germans, Dutch and Americans.

It may be the richest country in Africa, but labour costs are low, so maids, gardeners, cooks and other staff are not expensive. But by far the most important factor attracting prospective homebuyers to South Africa, certainly until recently, has been the large and advantageous contrast in property prices. However, the gap has narrowed recently, for two reasons. Not long after the millennium, South African residential prices in popular areas began to rise steeply. They increased by 30 per cent over two years, and in property hotspots rocketed by the same amount in one year. The other factor is the exchange rate. The pound has weakened against the South African rand in recent years, from a high of almost twenty rand to the pound at the end of 2001 to as low as twelve, two years later.

Even so, UK buyers continue to get a lot of property for their cash. There is plenty of property available without having a six-figure budget. And for those who decide to sell up in the UK in order to make a permanent move, there are enticing options.

For example: sell your UK home for £200,000 and you could buy its South African equivalent for less than half the price, and throw in a pool and garage for good measure. Then put the balance in a South African bank, and take advantage of the country's high interest rates in order to have a healthy annual income.

Or, given the volatility of the rand, some investors in SA property prefer to keep some of the balance in sterling, for example, in the form of an annuity or a pension. Alternatively, sell your UK home and use the cash to buy a sizeable property in South Africa, plus a small UK bolthole. And that South African purchase could be an income-generating property: for example, a guesthouse or B&B? A vineyard or small game farm? A haven for hikers and birdwatchers? Accommodation for sporting guests, such as golfers? These are all tried and tested business ventures.

types of property

Outside city centres, a typical mid-price range property is a three or four-bedroom bungalow, with double garage, swimming pool and large garden complete with outdoor *braai* (barbecue) and bougainvillea. In the better areas, you could pay

£25,000 either side of £100,000, which buys a lot of bricks and mortar compared with real estate in Britain.

In South Africa, perhaps to an even greater extent than in Britain, location is all. In some places, you could buy that property for not much more than £50,000. But add another nought if it were smartened up with a higher degree of finishing (expensive imports in the kitchen, for example) and were then transported to a prime site, with forests and mountains in the background, and views over golden sands wedged between the cliffs of a dinky secluded bay. There would be nothing wrong with the £50,000 house. It would be in a perfectly acceptable area, perhaps within a mile or two of its more expensive twin, but it would not have that to-die-for scenery.

Although the rest of South Africa has its attractions (and a few places you would rather not go to at all), it is **Cape Town** that springs to mind first for property-seeking foreigners. It is a generic term which not only encompasses the city, but also the outlying areas, especially the Atlantic Seaboard suburbs to the north and the Southern Suburbs.

Cape Town itself combines modern and historical architecture. Much of it is situated in the recently revitalized downtown waterfront area, close to the central business district. Gone, though, are the days when you could pick up small seaview apartments for £50,000.

A one-bedroom apartment in a new glass-fronted luxury development, or a loft in a refurbished existing commercial building, can cost as much as a free-standing family house in outlying suburban districts where traditional buildings sit happily alongside modern villas and architect-designed houses.

The word 'suburb' does not have the same pejorative connotations as it does in the British property market. The Southern Suburbs, Constantia, Newlands and Rondebosch are desirable areas to live in, especially in **Upper Constantia** where a palatial property, whether classic Cape Dutch or cutting-edge modernity amid lush greenery, can approach the £1,000,000 mark. But it is still possible to step onto the lower rungs of the local property ladder at a tenth of the price.

Slightly further afield, travelling south along the Atlantic, is the stretch of coastline, reaching down to the fishing port of **Hout Bay**, where the diversity of residential properties indicate the broad spectrum of lifestyles: equestrian estates, mansions, game reserve lodges, marina developments, reasonable family homes and lock-up-and-go apartments.

Along the way are **Bantry Bay**, with prestige apartment blocks, often supported on stilts and set into the mountain side, trendy **Clifton** and the broad sweep of **Camps Bay**, all with properties at the top end. You could fork out much more for a two-bedroom apartment or splash out for a glamorous mansion, pool and staff quarters, set in lush gardens – all priced according to location and view.

Further to the east, but still well within striking distance of the city, is the **Cape Winelands** area, where small vineyards come onto the market as going concerns for the price of a substantial London house, as well as B&Bs and small farms for

considerably less. Many of the properties are beautiful houses in styles inherited from the country's colonial past, especially Cape Dutch or early Victorian with wraparound verandas.

Away from the tourist mecca of Durban's sea front lie quiet suburbs basking under the tropical sun.

Cape Dutch architecture, based on the Baroque architecture of Holland, evolved from the mid-eighteenth century when it began as a simple row of thatched rooms. Its most prominent features are end gables to protect the roof from being blown away in high winds, and the front end gable which is a device to build a window in the reed thatch above the front door to allow light into the attic. Traditional Cape Dutch houses also have whitewashed walls and sash windows made of small panes.

Georgian houses, with gently sloping tile roofs, precise brick work, louvred shutters to exclude strong sunlight and a lobby at the front entrance to prevent draughts, came along at much the same time. This was followed by a variation of Victorian architecture, often in terraced rows, with ornamental gables and stained glass windows. There is usually a front veranda with cast iron pillars supporting the corrugated iron awning fringed with intricate cast iron detail.

Another popular area among British and other foreigners is the **Garden Route**, the forest-fringed southern coastline extending from the Western Cape well into the Eastern Cape. It is handily situated along the N2 motorway between Cape Town international airport, a few hours drive to the west, and the internal airport of Port Elizabeth to the east with the smaller airport of George situated midway.

The 500 kilometres or so between Mossel Bay and Jeffrey's Bay, with its dramatic variety of beach, forest and lakes, are studded with holiday homes owned by wealthy city-dwellers beyond the pocket of the average South African, but often well within reach of the foreign buyer. Even so, if these prices seem daunting, there is an abundance of more affordable properties which seem cheap in comparison with the UK and are proving attractive to the British seeking a retirement home in the sun.

For example, while the smarter resorts such as **Plettenberg Bay** (think of Padstow in Cornwall or Burnham Market in Norfolk) are pricey, within a mile or so you can still find a three-bedroom house, with garden and double garage, for well below £75,000. **Knysna** is just one of the resorts tipped as a good place to invest, with excellent buy-to-let opportunities. Throughout the region, one-storey detached houses – the norm in South Africa outside cities – are popular, as are timber lodges in rustic log-cabin style, with wraparound verandas.

Another area luring buyers from abroad is the **Hibiscus Coast**, an hour-and-a-half south of Durban in KwaZulu-Natal, high up on the east coast of South Africa. Here, for less than the price of a seaside studio flat in Spain (and half the price of comparable properties in Cape Town), villas are on the market with pool and all the attractions of outdoor living, including miles of secluded beaches along the warm Indian Ocean.

Towns such as **Scottburgh** are popular holiday resorts for locals, and it is here among the costa-style developments that real bargains (under £50,000) are to be found, although they might not be the kind of properties that appeal for year-round living. The coast north of Durban – **Umhlanga** and **Ballito**, for example – is becoming increasingly popular among investors looking for a healthy return on their outlay.

KwaZulu-Natal, often referred to as the last English outpost thanks to its colonial feel, is a mecca for golfing enthusiasts. A growing trend here, as elsewhere in South Africa, is to buy a house or apartment on a securely gated golf course complex. The demand for golf estate living continues unabated, not only for lifestyle reasons, but also because recently they have proved an outstanding return on investment – in some cases up by 30 per cent in a year. Wealthy South Africans often snap up one of these developments off-plan as soon as they go on the market – even if they don't play golf.

points to consider

However diverse the properties throughout the country, the one thing they are likely to share is a degree of security, often including high walls, secure garages and electronic gates. Most homes are equipped with security devices and many homeowners have contracts with armed response security companies or live in neighbourhoods patrolled by armed guards. That said, observers claim that high crime levels are restricted to small areas, and provided one takes sensible precautions, it is not as bad as the outside world perceives it.

To meet demand, more and more gated communities – or 'cluster homes' – are being built, often with communal facilities such as a swimming pool, and are subject to a monthly community charge. Before buying, it's essential to check what the charge is and exactly what it covers.

price bands

Note: Prices at Spring 2004 exchange rate: approx £1 = R12. Remember: these prices are a rough guide and can vary enormously, even within a small location. *Key*: CT = Cape Town. GR = Garden Route. HC = Hibiscus Coast.

below £50,000
- rare, but possible, for small one-bed cottage or KwaZulu-Natal coast holiday flats

£50,000–£75,000
- basic three-bed bungalow in GR suburb, no view
- two-bed retirement home on secure GR estate
- starting price for good two-bed city apartment
- four-bed, two-bathroom HC bungalow

£75,000–£100,000
- two-bed Cape Dutch-style cottage, GR or CT suburb
- large plot on game reserve (ex building cost)

Cape Dutch houses characterize a street in Tulbagh in the Western Cape.

- basic three- or four-bedroom family house most areas
- small seaview apartment, CT

£100,000–£125,000
- luxury bungalow on CT golf estate, bigger on HC
- two-bedroom apartment in smart CT beachfront block
- four-bed house, possible pool, granny flat, all areas
- small farmhouse or B&B

£125,000–£175,000
- four-bed house, pool etc. in smart GR or CT suburb
- three-bed three-bath timber house on secure GR complex
- four-bedroom inland HC house, pool, extensive land
- luxury GR apartment, garage, superb views

£175,000–£225,000
- as above, with extras – e.g. staff pool, extra bedroom, views

£225,000–£400,000
- GR guesthouse, seven en suite bedrooms, near beach
- four- or five-bed house, pool, garden in smart CT suburb
- CT apartments, according to location and view

£400,000+
- luxury homes and apartments in exclusive CT, GR and HC locations
- lifestyle estates (game reserves, vineyards, sports), some with potential income

Buying property in South Africa Q&A

Buying property is a complex process. To ensure that things go as smoothly as possible, be sure to take appropriate professional advice on both legal and financial matters. What follows is a brief introduction to what you can expect to find.

Q How do I choose an estate agent?

A Finding an estate agent is done just as it is in the UK via the Internet, local newspapers, property magazines, For Sale/Sold signs and their local offices. A precaution is to check that they are a registered member of the Estate Agency Affairs Board, possessing a current fidelity fund certificate (they expire at the end of each year).

Q What is the Estate Agency Affairs Board?

A The EAAB was set up in accordance with the Estate Agency Affairs Act 1976 to regulate the estate agency industry. Their role is to protect the public's interest, making sure all estate agents meet agreed standards either by taking an exam or undergoing a year's practical training with a qualified agent and that they adhere to the Code of Conduct. The Board will investigate complaints against estate agents, imposing sanctions on them if it's found they've violated the Code of Conduct, and will reimburse customers who have suffered financial loss through such misconduct from the Fidelity Fund.

Q Can I take out a mortgage in South Africa?

A Yes. But a bank can only lend a non-resident up to the equivalent of the amount they are putting in themselves, i.e. up to 50 per cent of the purchase price. Any loan has to be approved by the South African Reserve Bank that can be obtained through any South African Commercial Bank offering financial assistance.

Q How will Exchange Control affect me?

A Although Exchange Control is going through a process of deregulation to encourage foreign investment, it is still a complex subject. If you are planning to buy a home in South Africa, it is worth seeking professional advice as regards your individual circumstances, particularly since the exchange controls are liable to change. To bring money into the country for the purchase of your property you will have to declare your intentions to the South African Bank.

Q Can I repatriate the funds I brought to SA for the purchase if I sell the property?

A You can repatriate both your funds and any profit.

Q Once I've found a property should I get it surveyed?

A It is not standard practice in South Africa to conduct property surveys. Of course it is always a wise precaution and can be arranged either through the estate agent or lawyer. If you decide to commission one, make sure it is included in the Agreement of Sale as a condition of the purchase and that it is made clear the survey will cover the structure of the building (in South Africa a 'survey' usually refers to surveying the land and establishing the property boundaries).

Q Should I engage a solicitor?

A The general rule is that the seller chooses the transferring attorney, but it is always worth engaging your own solicitor to protect your interests when dealing with the legal intricacies of a property purchase. Ensure that your solicitor specializes in conveyancing and is based in the Republic of South Africa. Your solicitor's expertise may save you considerably more than the fee.

Q What is an Offer to Purchase?

A Once an offer is made the estate agent completes an Offer to Purchase or Agreement of Sale form, which must be signed by both parties or their representatives in order to be binding. This form may be particular to that estate agency or, alternatively, a standard form is available from the EAAB and it must contain all the material terms of the sale. The details should be thoroughly checked by the purchaser and the seller before signing, preferably in conjunction with their lawyers. A number of points must be included:

● the deeds office description of the property including the residential address, the agreed purchase price and the full names and relevant details of all parties in the transaction;

● fixtures and fittings, e.g. whether or not the carpets or curtains or specific pieces of furniture are included in the sale; this should be as clear and as unambiguous as possible so there are no misunderstandings;

● if the purchaser is dependent on getting a loan or mortgage within a certain period of time, this should be specified;

● the agreed date when the purchaser can move in;

● if there are any patent defects in the property they should be mentioned as well as whether or not the seller is going to rectify them;

● *voetstoots* – 'as is' – this means that the seller can't be held responsible for any hidden defects of which s/he is unaware;

● the agreed estate agent's commission; as the purchaser, make sure there's no provision for you to pay the agent a commission from your deposit; this is usually paid by the seller;

● if the sale is dependent on the purchaser's current property being sold, a date should be included by which it is done; take advice from your solicitor about the careful wording of this clause;

● if the property purchase price is less than R250,000, a cooling-off period may apply (i.e. giving the purchaser the right to revoke his agreement within an agreed amount of time after signing the agreement or offer), and its length and expiry date should be included in the agreement;

● electrical and beetle-free certificate; every South African property owner must have a certificate confirming that all electrical installations at the property meet statutory safety requirements; similarly there is a certificate to guarantee the property is free from infestation, but this is not compulsory; the buyer should insist on the beetle-free certificate and make it a specific condition of

sale if there is a lot of woodwork in the property, such as wooden floors;

● any other conditional clauses relating to the sale.

Situated on the banks of the Swartkops River estuary, Amsterdamhoek is ideal for those who like birding, water sports and magnificent sunsets.

Q Do I pay a deposit and what happens to it?

A On signature of the Offer to Purchase or Agreement of Sale, a deposit of 10 per cent is usually payable to the transferring attorney or conveyancer representing the seller who will hold it in a trust account until the sale is completed and the property is registered in the name of the new owner. This deposit is not a legal requirement but is a gesture of good faith on the part of the buyer.

Q What is a conveyancer?

A In South Africa, registrations of mortgage and property transfers are conducted by a conveyancer, i.e. an attorney who specializes in property law. When s/he receives the agreement, s/he is responsible for checking it and for preparing the transfer documents that, once signed by buyer and seller, are lodged with the new mortgage bonds in the regional Deeds Registry. It is the conveyancer who attends the Deeds Registry offices and signs the deeds passing transfer from the seller to the purchaser before the Registrar of Deeds.

Q What happens at the Deeds Registry?

A The deeds are scrutinized then made available for registration. This normally takes between eight and ten working days. On the day of the transfer of the property, all the old mortgage bonds are cancelled and the new ones, if any, are registered in favour of the bank issuing the loan. This is a complicated process and ownership of the property only transfers with its completed registration (six to eight weeks after signature of the Agreement of Sale).

Q Are there any additional costs?

A Yes. The additional costs are as follows:

- transfer costs are payable to the Receiver of Revenue and include transfer duty calculated as follows:

  R0 – R150,000 – exempt

  R150,001 – R320,000 – 5 per cent

  R320,001 and over – 8 per cent or 10 per cent for companies and close corporations.
- conveyancer's fees (calculated according to a standard tariff), usually about 1–2 per cent of the purchase price;
- mortgage costs;
- estate agents commission; usually paid by the seller unless mutually agreed otherwise.

The vast expanses and big skies of the Eastern Cape attract those who want to live off the beaten track.

Q How long will the sale take to go through?

A Usually between six weeks to three months.

Q Can I let my property?

A Yes. The rental income will be taxable by the South African government. It is your responsibility to register as a taxpayer.

Q Do I need a visa or residency permit?

A British citizens do not need a visa to enter South Africa. On arrival, you will receive a three-month permit that is extendable for three months at a time as long as you have evidence you can support yourself during that time, have a return ticket or funds to buy one and apply no less than thirty days before the previous one expires. Apply to a District or Regional Office of the Department of Home Affairs.

If, however, you plan to move to South Africa permanently, there are different residency permits available. The appropriate one should be applied for from your country of residence. However, you may apply from within the country if: you are in South Africa and have a valid work permit; are married to or are the child of a South African citizen or permanent resident and; you have a valid temporary residence permit and are being sponsored by a family member who is a permanent resident; you've been exempted from holding a temporary residence visa. The fact that you are intending to or have bought a house does not affect your application. The four most relevant permanent residence permits are: retired person's; financially independent; work; business. The following is a brief guide:

Retired persons permits

The applicant must be able to prove they have a net worth of R12 million that provides a monthly income of R150,000. Otherwise they must have an annuity or retirement account that provides at least R20,000 per month. If these criteria are fulfilled, they can stay in South Africa for four years on a seasonal or continuous basis. The application must be made from abroad. Fee R1,520.

Financially independent

This applies to wealthy applicants who can prove a net worth of R20 million and pay an application fee of R100,000. A certain sum will have to be invested in the South African economy for three years, e.g. buying property or depositing the sum in a bank. Under this visa, the applicant is not allowed to set up their own business or take employment without approval of the Department of Home Affairs.

Work permits

To apply for a work permit, you must have a job offer before your arrival and must apply from abroad. Employers have to show that they have advertised the post in South Africa and have been unable to find a suitable candidate. In the case of certain skills or qualifications, this condition may be waivered. If professionally qualified, you must register with the equivalent SA bodies. Fee R1,520.

Business permits

The South African government is keen to encourage investment in the country so those with business plans that involve an investment of R2.5 million and employment opportunities for South Africans will be granted a two-year permit. They will also have to show they can support themselves and family during this time. These conditions can be waived depending on the type of business and on the say-so of the Department of Trade and Industry. If you go into business with others or continue an established business, after one year, the Department of Home Affairs will expect to see proof that your role has led to a contribution to the country's economy or to the employment of two South Africans or more.

Living in South Africa

government and economy

On 27 April 1994, Nelson Mandela became South Africa's first democratically elected president. At last voters ended centuries of black oppression by the whites and overthrew the apartheid system that had kept the country isolated from the rest of the world for decades. The issues facing the government were huge – unemployment, poverty and disease perhaps being the three most pressing.

Two years later, the new constitution was agreed and ratified by the Supreme Court. The Parliament consists of two houses, the National Assembly and the Senate. The National Assembly is elected by a system of proportional representation while the Senate is chosen by the nine provincial assemblies that are locally elected, also by proportional representation: Eastern Cape, Free State, Gauteng, KwaZulu-Natal, Limpopo, Mpumalanga, North-West, Northern Cape, Western Cape. Somewhat controversially these days, Parliament sits in Cape Town while the government ministries are located in Pretoria. Plans are afoot to move the Parliament to Pretoria although unsurprisingly strenuous objections are heard among delegates from the Western Cape. In April 2004, the ANC was returned by its biggest majority yet under the leadership of President Thabo Mbeki who entered his second term of office.

Over the last twenty years, great strides have been made in areas of deprivation and the poorest now have running water and electricity. However there is still a huge gap between the wealthy and the poor, and resentment that things are not changing enough or fast enough has led to one of the government's greatest problems today – the high crime rate.

South Africa has vast mineral resources, most famously some of the world's largest gold and diamond mines as well, but is also a major producer of other minerals particularly platinum. Around 25 per cent of the labour force is tied up in industry, principally involved with mining, automobile assembly, metalworking, machinery, textiles, iron and steel, chemicals, fertilizer and foodstuffs; 30 per cent of the country's labour force is involved in agricultural production and ensures the country is self-sufficient, producing corn, wheat, sugarcane, fruits, vegetables; beef, poultry, mutton, wool, dairy products. Because of apartheid, South Africa is

only now beginning to be able to break into foreign export markets. Despite all efforts since 1994, growth has not been sufficient to lower the high unemployment rates. Poverty remains a problem along with crime and HIV/AIDS. Together, they have deterred foreign investors. Tourism is another growing source of income. With Rand falling in value against other foreign currencies, the cost of living is cheap for European and British immigrants.

The broad tree-lined streets of Grahamstown in the Eastern Cape are a legacy from the time it was the Cape's second city.

education

Education is available in South Africa from age five to eighteen. At present the reception year is not compulsory, and as in the UK, classes are run in most primary schools or in nursery schools. Primary education occupies grade one to six, followed by high school for grades seven to twelve. At present all grades from one to twelve are compulsory. In Grade nine they take the CTAs (Common Task Assessment) which qualifies them for the GETCs (General Education and Training Certificate). From 2006, this will be the exit point for those who don't want to continue. In Grade twelve (still known as Matric) they will take the FETs (Further Education and Training), and need to satisfy certain criteria in these to qualify for university. At present they're still taking the Senior Certificate exams in Matric, which varies slightly from province to province. Private schools also have to take these exams.

As everywhere, standards, ethos, size and financial resources in schools and universities in South Africa vary widely. At state schools, despite state funding, parents are expected to contribute some fees towards the basics and standards in some are on a par with the best private schools. Private education has existed in SA for many years, the schools having their origins in mission schools, and now caters for 2 per cent of the twelve million in school. There are over 1,000 registered private schools in the country with a number of unregistered ones operating as well.

health care

There are numerous private and public hospitals in South Africa and standards are high, particularly in relation to those in the rest of the continent. However there is a huge divide between the two sectors in terms of both facilities and funding. The state provides basic primary care but the most advanced medical treatment is available only for those who can afford it. South Africa does not have a national health system so patients are expected to pay for consultations and treatment. The private sector is growing rapidly and caters for about 20 per cent of the population. Doctors and hospitals expect immediate payment for their services and will accept credit cards. However by taking out private insurance, a consistently high level of health care and a personal service are ensured. For anyone buying a holiday home or moving there permanently, taking out private medical insurance is a must.

pets

Before any pet can be brought into the country, an import permit must be applied for from the Director of Animal Health in Pretoria. Application must be accompanied with a payment of R90. The permit will be sent to you with a Veterinary Health Certificate that must be completed by a government-authorized vet (LVI) within ten days of departure. These have to be presented at the Port of Entry along with any other specified forms such as an indemnity form or a rabies vaccination certificate. If the paperwork is not complete, a quarantine of sixty days will be imposed. For further details, visit www.nda.agric.za/vetweb.

You must ensure your pet is transported in an IATA (International Air Transport Association) approved air kennel that gives it room to stand and move around.

Note that South Africa is *not* a member of the government's Pets Travel Scheme (PETS), so if you only intend to stay in South Africa for a limited time, you will have to put your pet into six months' quarantine when it reaches the UK. For further detailed information, visit www. defra.gov.uk.

driving

South Africans drive right-hand drive cars on the left-hand side of the road. The wearing of seatbelts is compulsory. Using handheld mobile telephone while driving is against the law. An international driving licence is acceptable but permanent residents should acquire a South African driving licence within six months of moving. General speed limits are 75mph on national highways, 65mph on secondary roads and 35mph in built-up areas. International road signs are used with distances in kilometres. There are toll roads on certain highways. The petrol stations are not self-help and usually payment is expected in cash.

car

If you are a first-time immigrant to South Africa, you are allowed to import one car per household under rebate of duty, provided you have owned it for more than one year. A signed declaration form (DA304A) for motor vehicles must be presented when clearance is effected. First-time immigrants, must produce their Permanent Residence Permits. You will not be able to rent, sell, exchange your car for the first twenty months you're in the country without approval of the Commissioner for the South African Revenue Service and payment of outstanding duties.

taxation

All income earned in South Africa is subject to income tax, including rental income from a property. Income below R30,000 or R47,222 (if you are over 65) is tax free. Other than that you will be charged tax according to published tax tables up to a maximum rate of 40 per cent. Workers are taxed on a PAYE basis, levied on a sliding scale.

Capital gains tax was introduced to South Africa in 2001. For private individuals the rate is 25 per cent. Exemptions do exist for non-residents so it is worth taking independent financial advice.

For detailed information on taxation in South Africa, visit the South African Revenue Service at www.sars.gov.za.

House-hunters

Cape Town

Frank and Jane O'Connor
Budget: **approx £60,000**

Above: Cape Town. Historic two-bedroom cottage with large living/dining area, kitchen and bathroom; courtyard, secure parking and front garden: £42,000.

Below: False Bay. Rustic hideaway with three en suite bedrooms, lounge/dining room, family room and kitchen; pool, garage, garden: £76,000.

Regular holidays in Cape Town had given sales manager, Frank O'Connor, and his wife Jane a taste for a new life. They never tired of the scenery and awe-inspiring mountains and never looked forward to going home. Their plan was to find a holiday home that they could rent out when not staying in it themselves.

The first house they saw was a traditional one-hundred-year-old Cape cottage in the cultural centre of **Cape Town**. Deceptively small from the outside, the hall opened into a high-ceilinged open-plan living/dining area. The compact kitchen was fully fitted with everything they needed. The master bedroom had a large north-west facing window that let in lots of light, and louvred wardrobes providing plenty of storage. The modern tiled bathroom was surprisingly large for such a small property. Outside the courtyard proved to be the ideal space for relaxing in a hammock or for a barbecue. Both Frank and Jane were entranced by the cottage, loving its character, space and location. It seemed ideal as a holiday property because it would be so easy just to lock up and go without worrying about security or a garden. They were interested to learn that they could expect a rental income of £300 per month which would represent a significant return on their investment. One idea would be to advertise in a book, *The Whole Lot*, which lists accommodation for people in the film business.

Next they headed to **False Bay**, an area increasingly popular with British buyers. There was an attractive house in a complex overlooking the bay. Combining rustic features such as terracotta tiles and exposed beams with modern design features, this house seemed to offer the best of both worlds. The main living/dining area was large and bright with french windows leading to the pool area. Just off it was a family area with an open brick fireplace for cool winter nights. The small well-equipped kitchen complete with Belfast sink had a country feel. Upstairs were two bright and cosy guest bedrooms with en suite bathrooms. The huge master bedroom led out onto a spacious veranda with spectacular views of the mountains. The walk-in wardrobe was large enough to be converted into a fourth bedroom while the en suite tiled bathroom featured a modern circular shower. Outside there was a triple garage, modest front and back garden with a terracotta veranda, the main selling point being the large outdoor pool. The O'Connors hadn't previously considered living in a gated community but could see the benefits it offered: security; a good social scene; well-maintained communal areas. A £15 monthly charge covered the maintenance of those areas, including the street lighting, roads, private security company and rubbish collection. Despite appreciating the advantages, they felt it wasn't right for them and disliked the fact they would need a car to get anywhere.

They continued their search in **Hout Bay**. Here, there was a detached villa on a complex that seemed to offer all they wanted. The tiny hall led into a large airy reception with sliding doors leading to the patio. Linked to it through a hatch was the modern fully equipped kitchen. The cool master bedroom had a large white bathroom en suite and led onto a terrace. Surrounded by the Constantia mountains, this was a perfect location especially for enthusiastic walkers. Frank and Jane thought the villa was superbly designed and the sizes of the rooms were perfect. The potential rental of £420 during the summer rising to £800 over Christmas was an additional attraction.

Above: Hout Bay. Three-bedroom detached villa with open-plan living/dining room, kitchen, two bathrooms, under-floor heating; private garden: £60,000.

They finished their search in the countryside of the **Winelands** where a local artist had designed and built an ultra-modern house. Constructed from Perspex and steel, it was very different from the three previous properties and had even won a National Design Award. Very much the sort of property that arouses strong feelings, it offered a striking living space, a kitchen with doors leading onto the patio, an artist's studio that could be a living area. The white master bedroom was very peaceful and had an en suite bathroom with particularly little windows. Outside a fish pond was stocked with Koi carp and the plunge pool was blessed with its own dressing room. The O'Connors had to agree to disagree on this one. Jane loved it but Frank had a more pragmatic approach and felt strongly that, from a practical viewpoint, the house wouldn't represent a sound investment and might present problems when/if they decided to resell it since it would appeal to a limited market.

Below: Winelands. Award-winning three-bedroom designer house with open-plan living/dining/studio area, kitchen, three bathrooms; small garden and pool: £55,000.

After much discussion, they decided that although they loved the third property, the first they had seen in the centre of Cape Town presented the most ideal solution to their needs. They visited it for a second time and as a result put in an offer of £41,000 but unfortunately the vendor accepted a higher cash offer, leaving the O'Connors to continue their search.

House-hunters

Kevin and Adrian Hainsworth

Hibiscus Coast
Budget: **£200,000**

Holidaymakers find all they need on the coast south of Durban, yet at the same time there are miles of secluded beaches. Gardener Kevin Hainsworth and his brother Adrian, a salesman, had never been to South Africa when they

Above: Scottburgh. Five-bedroom Italianate villa with six bathrooms, two living rooms, kitchen; private pool, tropical greenhouse, servants' quarters, one acre of land: £55,000.

visited the area with the programme to look at properties there. They were aware that they would find much better value for money than they would in Europe and were looking for a three-bedroom villa with a pool and garden. They thought they would take it in turns to use the house since they both had big families although they also envisaged the occasional 'boys' holiday'. They were to be pleasantly surprised by what they found.

They started their hunt in the busy beach resort of **Scottburgh**, the first township established on the Hibiscus Coast, now a thriving resort renowned for its safe beaches. Here they viewed Wrose Wood Villa, a large Italianate property that bowled them over. It was arranged round a central ornamental courtyard with fountains and a fishpond. Inside the cool spacious living room benefited from windows along both sides and the brothers were particularly taken by the large modern kitchen with its long central island. The master bedroom was an impressive size too and led into its own en suite bathroom and greenhouse. If they paid an additional £3,000, the furniture would be thrown in. Outside, the tropical garden was an ideal size for the Hainsworth families. It was quite wild and home to a number of monkeys. Although many South Africans would consider them pests and fence the property to keep them out (£400), the brothers thought they were great. They were also encouraged to hear that the live-in maid and gardener who had worked on the property for seven years wanted to carry on for £50 and £40 per week, respectively. However they wondered whether it was in quite the right area for them.

Kevin and Adrian continued their search in **Southbroom**, one of the most upmarket areas on the Hibiscus Coast. Many Pretorians and Joburgers have holiday homes here. Set behind the sandy beach is the local golf course. Although property here is expensive by South African standards, it's still very affordable for British buyers. About thirty of them already own property in the area. The living area was simply vast, dwarfing even the full-size snooker table. A lot of natural wood was used in the design as it was in the kitchen that had a convenient hatch to the dining area. The house was once a B&B so each bedroom had its own en suite bathroom. The outside space was divided into a tropical garden and a rock-feature swimming pool for daytime use and a Jacuzzi for night-time. If the brothers wanted to continue the B&B, they were relieved to learn that, in South Africa, you are only expected to provide the bed but not the breakfast. For that, they could charge £25 per night without having to pay any extra fees or services and the Tourist Board would advertise it.

Southbroom. Seven-bedroom African-style lodge with seven en suite bathrooms, kitchen, open-plan living/dining/study/bar; pool, Jacuzzi, one acre of garden: £81,000.

Next they travelled inland to the **Midlands–Zulu** territory where, in 1879, British soldiers held out in the battle for Rourke's Drift. The mile upon mile of unspoilt countryside is loved by campers who head particularly for Midmar Lake, a popular watersports' centre. Built in 1884, a neo-classical

Victorian villa offered plenty of space for the Hainsworth families. It was originally commissioned by a family of tailors and was renovated twenty years ago. Laid out over one floor, this palatial home had high ceilings and retained many of its original features such as the hand-painted door panels. There were three kitchen areas, the largest of them being pretty basic. The magnificent living rooms still had their ornate cornicing while the bedrooms each had original wood-burning fireplaces. Both the master bedroom and the dining room had direct access to the grounds. Outside there was a large pool and a

Above: Midlands. Six-bedroom Victorian villa with three kitchen areas, dining room, two living rooms; separate four-bedroom cottage; landscaped garden, pool and tennis court: £125,000.

tennis court that needed resurfacing. The cottage, currently used as servants' quarters was larger than either of the brothers' homes back in Bradford. To renovate it into a guest house, including new ceilings, plasterwork, insulation, wiring and plumbing, would cost around £10,000. Another money-spinner would be to follow the current owner's trick of letting the house through a film location agency as a set for £200 per day. The only thing the Kevin and Adrian would have to bear in mind was the fact that, as it was a listed building, it might be difficult to make any alterations. They were tempted but felt that it was too far from the beach to have the sort of holiday feel they wanted.

Finally, they looked in **Margate**, a booming resort where property prices had doubled in the previous two years. Here they saw a seafront villa with a calm white-tiled interior that flowed from one living space into another. They were most impressed with the indoor pool that had its own bar right beside it and wonderful views of the garden that were shared by most of the rooms in the house. The separate apartment had an open-plan living/dining area with a bar. The kitchen boasted similar fixtures and fittings to the main house. Outside, the pool lay invitingly in the tropical garden close to the entertainment area. Through bushes at the bottom of the garden was an uninterrupted expanse of beach and fantastic sea views. The Hainsworths were advised that the prices of beachfront properties in the area were rising by 30 per cent per year so they almost certainly wouldn't lose

Below: Margate. Four-bedroom luxury seafront villa with open-plan design, indoor pool, jacuzzi, two sun terraces; separate three-bedroom apartment with its own bar; outdoor pool, private garden with beach access and barbeque area: £187,500.

out. They agreed that the space, quality and location were perfect. If they wanted to rent the house, they could expect to get £750 per week, i.e. £6,000–£7,500 per season while the apartment would let for £500 per week. Ultimately they decided that, compared with the other properties they'd seen, it didn't offer such good value for money.

Having agreed to make the decision without involving their wives, the brothers were able to move quickly. They loved the house done up in African style and could see themselves living a life of luxury there as well as picking up on good rental possibilities. Unfortunately their offer was rejected so they had to think again. Undaunted, they offered the asking price on Wrose Wood Villa in Scottburgh, the first property they'd

seen. To their delight it was accepted. The purchase went through without a hitch and now the Hainsworths own a superb holiday home that they rent out when not using it themselves. See www.southafricanvilla.com for details.

Ex-pat experience

Knysna, South Africa

Ailsa and John Edmonds

It took two years for retired policeman John Edmonds and his wife, Ailsa, to organize their move to South Africa. They had both got to know the country before they met, loving both it and the people, and were keen to retire there early so that they could spend more time together and with their daughters Eve (5) and Tori (16). Encouraged by their eldest son Ben (20) they made the move even though he had to stay behind to continue his training in the royal Navy.

'Knysna is one of South Africa's "safe havens",' says Ailsa, explaining their choice of destination. 'It's green, beautiful, very safe and very cosmopolitan. It also has very good schools which was important to us.' Their first attempt to buy ended in disaster. They trawled the Internet, made plans to view a property but it was sold two days before they got there. Disheartened, they almost gave up but Ailsa had befriended an estate agent who called to say a house was coming on the market that she knew they would love.

'This time we phoned and got the owners to sign an agreement saying they wouldn't sell the house until we got there ten days later. It was perfect, very sunny with plenty of space, five bedrooms, a pool and two self-contained cottages we plan to use for holiday lets.' It is in the suburb of Belvidere, 'quite English in look', where their typical white-and-green house is surrounded by a white open fence.

The Edmonds' sunny, five bedroom house in Belvidere.

It was a long task getting their visa. They used Four Corners Immigration in Cape Town. 'It was expensive but worth it because they removed all the pressure and knew exactly how to handle the paperwork.' Less successful was their experience of moving. 'The most traumatic aspect was the removal company. We went to three and chose them because their package seemed so professional. They seemed to have thought of everything but they lost things, including a rocking chair, packed badly and broke things, as well as failing to make the agreed dates. It was a nightmare. We paid a massive insurance premium but we were never offered compensation.'

For their first month in Knysna, they lived in a B&B, run by friends who introduced them to people. 'On Eve's first day at school, we were invited to a party by another mother who remembered what it was like to be a newcomer, and I met women who have become good friends.' Eve and Tori both joined a private school where the fees are more affordable than they would be in the UK. However, after a year, Tori transferred to the local state school as she didn't settle. 'I wanted the smaller classes and the additional attention that the private school offered but Tori was used to the English state school system and is now very happy and flourishing there.'

Even in the two years the Edmonds have been in Knysna, they have noticed the cost of living rise in response to its development as a tourist area. 'It has upset the locals sufficiently for them to want to institute loyalty card systems in the shops and restaurants. Having said that, it is still far cheaper than the cost of living in the UK.' Private medical insurance is expensive and care must be taken to ensure that it will cover all eventualities and not leave you with costly shortfalls. 'The standard of care in hospitals is nowhere near as good as it is in British private hospitals though it is better than the NHS,' explains Ailsa. 'You really think twice about a visit to the doctor since medication is so expensive too.'

The one thing the family are convinced by is the vast improvement in their quality of life. 'We wake up, looking out over the lagoon. There's space, glorious weather and the people are very relaxed and friendly. Yes, there is some crime but you only have to be as vigilant as you would be in certain areas of the UK. Generally, this is a much more laid-back environment where you have to adapt to "African time" where things don't get done as quickly as you might like.' For Ailsa the biggest downside to this existence has been leaving her family and friends back home. 'It's such a comfort to have friends who you have known for years. It takes a long time to build up that sort of intimacy.' But she is the only one of the family hankering for a bit of her old life. The others have embedded themselves into their new home and would have it no other way. And even Ailsa admits that after a six-week visit to the UK, she was dying to get back home.

'The standard of care in hospitals is nowhere near as good as it is in British private hospitals though it is better than the NHS.'

the Caribbean

Introduction

Palm-fringed beaches, crystalline seas, tropical sun, rum punches, steel bands, the reggae beat, flamboyant carnivals and a relaxed, hedonistic lifestyle. These are all part and parcel of any popular Caribbean fantasy. However, scratch the surface, and each island will reveal its own very individual identity.

Originally populated by the Amerindians, they were discovered in 1642 by Christopher Columbus who believed he'd reached the East Indies. When his mistake was realized, the islands were christened the West Indies. The Spaniards claim to them was challenged by other European powers but by 1700, the English, French and Dutch had successfully colonized their share of them, importing slaves from Africa. Squabbles over possession raged until the Treaty of Vienna in 1815 when the political map of the region was finally settled. Slavery was gradually abolished during the nineteenth century so labour was brought in from other sources, largely India and China. So, the Caribbean became the huge melting pot of cultures that is still apparent today. In 1804, Haiti gained its independence, followed by the Dominican Republic (1844) and Cuba (1898). Then, during the second half of the twentieth century, independence was granted to Jamaica, Trinidad and Tobago (1962) followed by Guyana and Barbados (1966), the Bahamas (1973), Grenada (1974), Dominica (1978), St Lucia and St Vincent and the Grenadines (1979), Antigua (1980), Belize (1981) and St Kitts and Nevis (1983).

In addition to those independent states, the Caribbean also includes the French overseas departments of Guadeloupe (including St Barts, and north St Martin) and Martinique, the UK dependencies of Montserrat and Anguilla with Saba, St Eustatius and South St Martin falling to the Netherlands.

Culturally, the islands still owe plenty to their colonial allegiances. French language, customs and food prevail in the French Antilles while Dutch prevails in the Netherlands Antilles. On the islands with a British heritage – Barbados, Trinidad – you will find British-style politics, Anglican churches and the familiar sound of leather on willow. Everywhere brilliant coloured houses in pinks, blues, reds and greens stand out under fruit-laden trees while the air reverberates with music. Among the islands there are some of the best snorkelling and dive sites in the world with wonderful opportunities for sailing and watersports. With this cultural diversity and geographical variations to draw on, each island has retained its particular character so it is a question of taking your pick. Old-world charm prevails in St Kitts and Nevis; Antigua is rich in colonial history and boasts a beach for every day of the year; famous as the 'Nature Island', Dominica has spectacular scenery perfect for hikers, divers and naturalists; Guadeloupe's intriguing blend of French, African and Indian cultures expresses itself in the Creole language and food; French to its backbone, Martinique is fabled as the 'Island of Flowers'; green and fertile, Montserrat was a magnet for early Irish settlers so it is hardly surprising it became known as the 'Emerald Isle'; St Lucia offers its own unique blend of French and

Previous page: Basking beside aquamarine seas with a glass of rum punch in the hand – that is what awaits in the Caribbean.

facts

puerto rico

Capital: San Juan

Area: 9,104 sq km

Highest point: Cerro de Punta (1,338 m)

Lowest point: Caribbean Sea (0 m)

Coastline: 501 km

Population: 3,885,810

Currency: US dollar

Time zone: GMT −5hrs

Electricity: 120V 60 Hz

Weights and measures: metric

Religions: Roman Catholic

Language: Spanish

Government status: Commonwealth

International dialling code: 00 1 787

National holiday: 25 July, PR Constitutional Day; 4 July, US Independence Day

A quiet place, Antigua's Falmouth Harbour has provided a safe anchorage since the days of the early colonists.

British influences; St Barts is almost Mediterranean in its look and atmosphere, while on the US Virgin Islands, it is still possible to glimpse residual touches of the previous Danish government.

The islands are composed of two main chains, the Greater and the Lesser Antilles. The Greater Antilles include Cuba, Jamaica, the Cayman Islands, Haiti and the Dominican Republic, Puerto Rico and the Virgin Islands. With less rain and flatter terrain, the Lesser Antilles are subdivided into the Leeward Islands – Anguilla, St Martin/St Maarten, St Barts, Saba, St Eustatius, St Kitts, Nevis, Antigua, Barbuda, Montserrat and Guadeloupe – and the Windward Islands – Dominica, Martinique, St Lucia, Barbados, St Vincent, the Grenadines and Grenada. Just off the Venezuelan coast lie the Dutch ABC islands of Aruba, Bonaire and Curacao and Trinidad and Tobago, while north of the Greater Antilles lie the Bahamas and the Turks and Caicos Islands.

All are blessed with year-round mild temperatures, although they are most pleasant from November to June. The hurricane season (July to November) may not always be as alarming as it sounds, but it will at least fulfil its promise of rain.

Unfortunately, it is impossible to cover every Caribbean island and their possibilities here. Instead, let's sample what some of the more popular ones have to offer.

puerto rico

In 1493 Puerto Rico was claimed by the Spanish Crown. Four hundred years of subsequent colonial rule saw the indigenous Indians disappear and the importation of African slave labour. Then, in 1898, at the end of the Spanish-

American War, the island was ceded to the USA. Today the island is a flamboyant mix of these cultural influences. The American way of life has brought it superb infrastructure and all the amenities demanded by twenty-first-century living. Yet its Spanish heritage is all too evident in the architecture, cuisine and music.

Also known as the Island of Enchantment, Puerto Rico enjoys a tropical climate. Inland lies the Cordillera Central affording views to both the Atlantic and Caribbean coasts. Its highlights include the El Yunque rainforest, a haven for walkers and naturalists and the Rio Camuy Cave Park, a vast subterranean cave system in the west of the island.

Of course the main attraction lies in the proliferation of beaches. The principal town is **San Juan**, on the north coast, notable for its seven-block-square historic quarter with steep narrow streets, paved with bluish-grey bricks, flanked by the pastel fronts and wrought-iron balconies of restored colonial buildings. Otherwise the town offers buzzing modern resorts with plenty of restaurants, chic shopping and nightlife on offer. **Ponce**, on the south coast, is the island's second city, also with a beautifully restored historical quarter and centred on the Plaza las Delicias with its cathedral and Town Hall. Along the south-west coast lie some of the most attractive beaches on the island, particularly popular is **Boquerón**. While on the north it's worth heading for **Luquillo**, a hub for all watersports enthusiasts.

San Juan has a reputation as the culinary capital of the Caribbean. Apart from international cuisine, there are traditional favourites to be found such as *asopao*, a gumbo made with chicken or shellfish, hearty fish or beef stews, *empanadillas* (wraps) and *tostones* (fried banana slices). The Puerto Ricans know how to enjoy themselves with a local festival to be found almost every week. For music lovers there is the Casals Music Festival (June) and the Puerto Rican Heineken Jazz Festival (May).

Visit http://welcome.topuertorico.org for tourist information.

us virgin islands

Christopher Columbus was so impressed by the beauty of the Virgin Islands that he named them after the legend of St Ursula and her 11,000 virgins. In 1666, the Danish established government of the western islands of **St Thomas**, **St John** and **St Croix** (rhymes with 'boy') until they sold them to the USA in 1917. Water is scarce here. The sun shines all year round interrupted by sharp, short-lived showers during the winter months. Despite American influence and the availability of international cooking, the Creole cuisine has held its own and can often be eaten outdoors or to the strains of calypso or a steel band.

Although benefiting from US investment, the three islands couldn't be more different. St Thomas is the most developed of the three. **Charlotte Amalie** is the main town and the focus for the big cruise ships. The Danish legacy of pastel-painted heritage houses, street names and driving on the left are constant reminders of the island's provenance. The coastline is ribboned with beach resorts, most with access to the superb dive sites, while inland lie secluded private hideaways.

facts

us virgin islands

Capital: Charlotte Amalie

Area: 352 sq m

Highest point: Crown Mountain (474 m)

Lowest point: Caribbean Sea (0 m)

Coastline: 188 km

Population: 124,780

Currency: US dollar

Time zone: GMT -5

Electricity: 110V 60Hz

Weights and measures: Metric

Religions: Baptist, Catholic, Episcopalian

Language: English (Spanish and Creole)

Government status: n/a

International dialling code: 00 1 340

National holiday: 27 March, Transfer Day

Around two-thirds of the smallest island of St John is taken up by the protected Virgin Islands National Park which extends into a marine park. This is a secluded hideaway where the relaxed main town of **Cruz Bay** surrounds the main harbour, with the village of **Coral Bay** at the other end of the island with private homes dotted discreetly in the woods. Surfing opportunities are best along the north coast on **Trunk Bay**, **Caneel Bay**, **Cinnamon Bay** in particular, while the south offers more sheltered beaches.

St Croix is the largest of the islands but surprisingly perhaps is much more peaceful than St Thomas. The landscape divides between the rainforest dominating the west and rolling beachscapes more reminiscent of Devon and Cornwall. The island has a rich Danish legacy, particularly in the two principal towns of Christiansted and Friedriksted. **Christiansted** was established in 1733 and named after the Danish king. Its arcaded houses, brightly painted with overhanging balconies are instant reminders of its past. Redeveloped in part after the 1995 hurricane, the town is a busy but pleasant shopping centre but also boasts the historic Fort Christiansvaern, original Lutheran churches, and plenty of bars, clubs and restaurants. The monthly 'jump-up' brings music and dancing to the streets of Christiansted. It lasts well into the night and is not to be missed. Outside the town are historic estates, plenty of beaches, resorts and opportunities for outdoor activities. Buck Island National Monument lies just off the north-eastern shore and provides a great beach and unbeatable snorkelling over the coral reef. **Friedriksted** is Christiansted's sleepy historic counterpart on the west side of the island known for its historic waterfront, Victorian homes and mahogany-furnished Catholic church. Close by lie the St George Botanic Garden and one of St Croix's best known restored eighteenth-century sugar plantations, the Estate Whim Plantation Museum.

See www.usvi.net for tourist information.

antigua

With St Kitts and Nevis to the north-west and Guadeloupe to the south, Antigua lies in the middle of the Leeward Islands. The stunning coastline, indented with over 300 idyllic beaches, more than compensates for its unspectacular, scrubby but pleasant interior, interrupted with ruined plantation mills. Antigua is a major yachting centre and every year hosts the international Antigua Race Week. The Carnival lasts from July to August. Local culinary specialities include ducana (sweet potato, coconut and spices), slatfish, pepperpot and goat stew. As on the other islands, there is plenty of tropical fruit and shellfish.

Spotted by Columbus in 1483, he named the island after the statue of the Virgin Mary in Seville Cathedral. Claimed for the British by Admiral Nelson in 1784, it remained under British administration until 1981, when it gained its independence with the neighbouring island of Barbuda. The British legacy is self-evident, not least in the Antiguan reputation for world-class cricket.

facts

antigua

Capital: St Johns

Area: 443 sq km

Highest point: Boggy Peak (405 m)

Lowest point: Caribbean Sea (0 m)

Coastline: 153 km

Population: 67,900

Currency: Eastern Caribbean $

Time zone: GMT -5

Electricity: 230V 60HZ

Weights and measures: Metric

Religions: Christian

Language: English

Government status: Constitutional monarchy with UK-style parliament

International dialling code: 00 1 268

National holiday: 1 November, Independence Day

Located on a hillside outside Falmouth, Antigua, this secluded property enjoys breathtaking views of the sea.

The only city on the island is **St John's**, the capital. It's a lively place with numerous restored and dilapidated historic buildings that coexist with modern developments. Deep Water Harbour, Heritage Quay and Redcliffe Quay have all been restored for tourist entertainment and shopping, contrasting with the busy activity of Market Street's more traditional Public Market. The skyline is dominated by the twin baroque towers of St John's Cathedral, the third church to be built on the site. Luxury cruise ships moor in the harbour, not far from the popular city beach. Top of the beach resorts must be **Dickenson Bay** and **Runaway Bay**, five kilometres north of the capital. The north-eastern coastline is battered by powerful Atlantic rollers so most visitors head for the calmer pleasures on the Caribbean coast where some of the finest beaches are to be found, among them Carlisle Bay, Darkwood Beach, Jolly Beach and Rendezvous Bay. Small settlements are scattered across the island. The top sightseeing spots are in the area of **Falmouth** and **English Harbour**, once the base for the British Navy at Nelson's Dockyard, now the hub of the yachting fraternity. Over the water from the Dockyard lie the ruins of Shirley Heights, home to the Sunday 'jump-up' and with splendid views across to Guadeloupe

See www.antigua-barbuda.org for tourist information.

guadeloupe

Guadeloupe and Martinique are the principal islands in the French Antilles. They became a French possession in 1653, having been annexed to France in 1674. The British and French fought repeatedly over the island until, in 1763, France abandoned its claims in Canada in exchange for Britain's recognition of French control of the islands.

facts

guadeloupe

Capital: Basse Terre

Area: 1,780 sq km

Highest point: Soufrière (1,484 m)

Lowest point: Caribbean Sea (0 m)

Coastline: 306 km

Population: 440,190

Currency: Euro

Time zone: GMT -5

Electricity: 220V 50Hz

Weights and measures: Metric

Religions: Roman Catholic

Language: French, Creole

Government type: n/a

International dialling code: 00 590

National holiday: 14 July, Bastille Day

The historic centre of Guadeloupe's Pointe-à-Pitre is Place de la Victoire where the the French defeated the British in 1794.

The French influence is evident everywhere giving the islands their distinctive charm. The official language here is French. Food is generally either French or Creole. Good food is taken seriously, popular dishes being *crabe farcis* (stuffed crabs), *blaff* (fish or shellfish stew) and *lambi* (conch) although you won't have to go far to find the French staples of good coffee, croissants and baguettes.

Guadeloupe is butterfly-shaped. The western Basse Terre is mountainous and forested with the Parc National de la Guadeloupe extending offshore from the mainland. The eastern Grande Terre is much flatter and more densely populated with much of the land devoted to sugar cane plantations, fruit and some livestock. The capital **Pointe-à-Pitre** lies almost dead centre. This is the colourful entry point to the island thronging with traffic, its quay lined with noisy markets. Most of the original buildings were destroyed by the 1843 earthquake so while the narrow streets do feature some colonial houses, a lot of modern concrete buildings are in the mix.

Le Gosier is where the heart of the tourist industry beats. Smart gated hotels and man-made beaches are in awkward contrast to the neighbouring Caribbean village. The best beach is offshore on the Ile de Gosier. Nearby is the Aquarium, the largest in the Caribbean. On the road east to the small French West Indian village of **Ste Anne**, most headlands sport holiday-complex developments. The atmospheric town of **St-François** has a smart marina providing restaurants, cafés and retail therapy. Of all the villages this side of Guadeloupe, the most attractive must be **Port Louis** with its picture-perfect wooden colonial houses and long, immensely popular swathe of sand, the Plage du Soufleur.

In the west, Basse Terre is the administrative capital overshadowed by the steaming La Soufrière volcano. It's an attractive port town with French colonial buildings gathered round shady squares. The best beaches of Basse Terre are strung along the north-west coast at Ferry, Grande Anse and the black-sanded Plage Malendure with its nearby top dive site. **Deshaies** is Basse Terre's most attractive village, its wooden houses gathered around its harbour. Nearby is the superb Jardin Botanique de Deshaies. On this side of the island there are signposted walks and trails through the national park. From the top of La Soufrière are wide views over the island and out to sea.

As on the other Caribbean islands, the climate is balmy, the rum is good, the atmosphere laid back and the opportunities for water activities or just lazing in the sun are legion.

See www.frenchcaribbean.com for tourist information.

martinique

Famous for its exotic flowers, its beaches and beautiful women, Martinique is another jewel in the Caribbean crown. Its scenery is dramatic, the rain forests and mountains of the north dominated by Mont-Pelée with sugar cane grown in the south, the area most developed for tourism. The island's profusion of vegetation results from the relatively high rainfall with the wet season running from June to late November. Local festivals occur throughout the year, the most spectacular involving yole races (boats with coloured sails and teams of oarsmen) but also watch out for Mardi Gras, Ash Wednesday and Easter parades.. There are plenty of opportunities to try the mainstay of spicy Creole cooking or French cuisine wherever you are on the island.

During the seventeenth century, the capital of the island **Fort-de-France** was built around the Fort St-Louis that still operates as a military base. Today the heart of the city is its crowded waterfront and the central park of La Savane although suburbs spread into the surrounding hills. There is little to detain sun lovers here. They tend to head for the white sanded beaches in the south of the island. Napoleon's Empress Josephine was baptized in the church at **Les Trois-Ilets** with its pretty main square. Close by is the island's only eighteen-hole golf course. A little further on is the frenetic tourist centre of **Pointe du Bout**, complete with luxury hotels, marina and Creole village – the most expensive area on the island. The south coast is laced with beaches, one of the most heavenly being Pointe du Diamant just below the blue and coral houses of **Diamant** itself. Martinique's most southern village is the seaside town of **Sainte-Anne** with its two small squares, and streets that overlook the shady beach.

North of Fort-de-France lie a string of fishing villages, black-sanded beaches and old sugar plantations. The scenery of the interior is dramatic and mountainous with cascading waterfalls, thick forest interrupted by small villages such as **Morne-Rouge** (nearest the top of Mont-Pelée) and old sugar plantations. The former capital, **St Pierre**, is forever petrified after Mont-Pelée erupted in 1902, killing all the 30,000 inhabitants except for one man imprisoned in the local jail whose cell walls withstood the heat. Some of the island's oldest coastal villages are on the northern coast, among them **Le Pecheur**, once home of Mme de Maintenon, mistress to the French king, Louis XIV. Passing the pineapple plantations around Basse Pointe, the Atlantic coast is dramatic but the beaches too treacherous for swimming. **La Trinité** boasts a fine promenade, fronted by nineteenth-century and modern buildings looking out towards the Caravelle Peninsula. This spit of land

facts

martinique
Capital: Fort-de-France

Area: 1,100 sq m

Highest point: Montagne Pelée

Lowest point: Caribbean Sea 0m

Coastline: 350 km

Population: 425, 966

Currency: Euro

Time zone: GMT -5

Electricity: 220V 50Hz

Weights and measures: Metric

Religion: Roman Catholic

Language: French, Creole

Government status: n/a

International dialling code: 00 596

National holiday: 14 July, Bastille Day

has remained unspoilt. Threaded with walking trails, there is only one fishing village, **Tartane**, overlooking its own beach with several others nearby that are particularly popular with surfers.

See www.frenchcaribbean.com for tourist information.

dominica

Unlike many of the Caribbean islands, Dominica (pronounced Domineeka) has few beaches. The most striking are on the often unsafe-for-swimming Atlantic coast. Instead it is noted for its rugged landscape, challenging hiking country and top-rated dive sites. Parks and nature reserves protect much of the forested interior that rises to its highest point of Morne Diablotin in the north. The geography of the island demands that the inhabitants live in pockets, mostly by the Caribbean Sea. The island has not been developed for mass tourism so it still provides a unique getaway into nature.

Dominica lay ignored by marauding colonial powers until the 1720s when the British and French fought over its ownership, finally settling possession by the British in 1805. Despite being an independent member of the British Commonwealth, the island still exhibits a strong French influence. It is among poorest islands in the Caribbean, the terrain prohibiting the development of any large estates although there are many small holdings. The official language is English. The last two weeks of Lent sees the Carnival when streets are packed with pageants and the sound of calypso. A Dive Fest takes place in June while October is the time for the Creole Music Festival. The local cuisine is unpretentious. The national dish is mountain chicken (frogs' legs) with Creole staples such as callaloo soup, fried chicken and *rotis* (stuffed pancakes).

The capital **Roseau** in the south-west, lies on a small flat piece of coast. Its attraction lies in the weatherbeaten Creole buildings with their verandas suspended over the street, tin roofs, louvred windows and, in some cases, original gingerbread fretwork. The colonial heart of the town is the Old Market Place where slave auctions were once held, now a pedestrian precinct and shopping area.

North of the capital, there are beaches close to the towns of **Portsmouth** and **Mero** with fishing hamlets scattered along on the coast. Inland, small villages cling to mountainsides. On the

Dominica's second town, Portsmouth, is attractively situated on St Rupert's Bay.

north-east of the island lies Carib Territory where the last remaining tribe live on a 3,700-acre reserve. South of Roseau, lies the Morne Trois Pitons National Park, a UNESCO World Heritage Site, that includes the memorably named Emerald Pool, Boiling Lake and Valley of Desolation. On the coast sit charming seaside villages including **Soufrière**, named after the nearby sulphur springs, and **Scott's Head**, an attractive fishing village in a beautiful setting against the mountains.

See www.ndcdominica.dm for tourist information.

barbados

The most easterly island in the Caribbean and one of the most popular, Barbados has a well-developed coastline and a rural interior with rolling fields of sugar cane, sheep and sleepy villages. As with most of the islands, the calmest waters are on the west coast where top beaches such as Sandy Bay, Paynes Bay and Mullins Bay can be found. There's great surfing on the east coast and wonderful reef-diving on the west as well as endless opportunities for watersports.

The island was claimed by the British in 1625 and, thanks to its location, avoided the Anglo-French conflict and enjoyed an uninterrupted period of British rule until it gained its independence in 1966. The national passion for cricket is part of a colonial legacy of impressive plantation homes, cane fields and familiarly English place names. The traditional Crop Over Festival in July is the island's biggest, marking the end of the sugar cane harvest. Not to be forgotten are the Holetown Festival (February), commemorating the arrival of the British on the island, the Oistins Fish Festival (Easter) and a number of international sporting events that pepper the year. Apart from inevitable international cuisine that includes much

facts

dominica

Capital: Roseau

Area: 754 sq km

Highest point: Morne Diablotin (1,447)

Lowest point: Caribbean Sea (0 m)

Coastline: 148 km

Population: 69,655

Currency: East Caribbean $

Time zone: GMT -5

Electricity: 230V 50Hz

Weights and measures: Metric

Religion: Roman Catholic

Language: English, French patois

Government status: Parliamentary democracy, republic within the commonwealth

International dialling code: 00 1 767

National holiday: 3 November, Independence Day

Bridgetown, Barbados, shows its British heritage with areas named Strathclyde and Weymouth. It even has a Trafalgar Square, with a statue of Lord Nelson.

facts

barbados

Capital: Bridgetown

Area: 431 sq km

Highest point: Mount Hillaby (336 m)

Lowest point: Atlantic Ocean (0 m)

Coastline: 97 km

Population: 277,264

Currency: Barbadian dollar

Time zone: GMT -5

Electricity: 115V 50Hz

Weights and measures: Metric

Religions: Protestant

Language: English

Government type: Parliamentary democracy, independent sovereign state within the democracy

International dialling code: 00 1 246

National holiday: 30 November

local seafood, the local Bajan and Caribbean specialities include flying fish, *cou-cou* (corn and oatmeal pudding), *cohobblo pot* (spicy meat stew) and saltfish.

Bridgetown is the vibrant capital of the island where about half the population live. Action centres on the Careenage, busy hub of the sailing community. Among the modern buildings, the town's history is seen in the attractive colonial buildings, monuments and the old city. The island is divided into eleven parishes. The south coast resorts mostly fall under Christ Church. The further from Bridgetown the less developed they tend to be. **Rockley** and **Worthing** have great beaches; **St Lawrence Gap** is known for its hectic nightlife; **Maxwell** is mostly residential and has a couple of good beaches; **Oistins** is the centre of the local fishing industry; **Silversands** is a magnet for windsurfers. The west coast has been dubbed the Platinum Coast and is the islands prime resort area where the white-sanded beaches are the main attraction. **Holetown** is the oldest town on the island in the heart of the tourist industry and the parish of St James.

See www.barbados.org for tourist information.

trinidad and tobago

Once part of the South American mainland, Trinidad and its smaller sister island Tobago are the most southerly islands of the Lesser Antilles. Spanish settlers arrived in 1592, encouraging French catholic planters to join them in 1783. However the British took over in 1797 and eventually experimented with the island, ruling it from Britain but governing it with French and Spanish law. With the abolition of slavery came an influx of Indian labour, something that has contributed to its complex cultural mix. This dynamic island lives to an energetic beat that climaxes at Carnival Time when the capital Port of Spain throbs with music and revellers. The cuisine is a stew-pot of influences. The national dish is *callaloo* which is eaten with other Creole favourites, although don't be surprised to find Indian or Chinese specialities too. Once known as the Land of the Hummingbird, the island is a naturalist's dream, crowded with butterflies, birds and indigenous plants.

Colourful **Port of Spain** is characterized by its heaving streets, its noise, its architectural mix of modern, splendid colonial and typical West Indian buildings, its street traders and traffic. Outside the town, beach tourism has not been as heavily developed as in Tobago. Those in the north are the most popular, particularly **Maracas Bay** while the others get progressively quieter east of **Blanchisseuse**. Behind the coast lies the Northern range, cloaked in rain forest and site of the Asa Wright Nature Centre, a few kilometres on from Arima. One of the most attractive seaside resorts on this coast is **Grande Rivière** with a good stretch of beach where leatherback turtles return to nest. Most of the island's African population live in **Arima** and **St Joseph** both located with other towns along the Eastern main road, running from Port of Spain to the East coast. The south of the island is less populated than the north, with tourists only heading down to the Devil's Woodyard, site of mud volcanoes, and Pitch Lake, a lake of hot tar. In the south-west lie the plentiful oil and gas reserves that do so much for the island's

economy. Apart from the northern and central mountain ranges, the landscape is one of rolling hills and plains, scattered with small farming communities.

See www.visittnt.com for tourist information.

Pigeon Point is Tobago's best-known beach – a great place to watch the sun go down.

The property market

Piggybacking on their popularity as an affordable tourist destination, the Caribbean islands are proving increasingly attractive as somewhere to buy a second home. Once the preserve of the rich and famous, they now set out their stall for middle-income earners who discover their delights on holiday and then decide to buy a permanent stake on a paradise island.

When Christopher Columbus fetched up in the Caribbean in 1492, he wrote: 'I saw so many islands that I hardly knew how to determine to which I should go first.' Were he to return today, he would be equally struck by the diversity of properties on offer by estate agents.

The architecture of the archipelago's islands – some fronting up the wild Atlantic, some sheltering in the lee – has evolved not only because of the prevailing weather,

facts

trinidad & tobago

Capital: Port-of-Spain

Area: 5,128 sq km

Highest point: El Cerro de Aripo (940 m)

Lowest point: Caribbean Sea (0 m)

Coastline: 362 km

Population: 1,104,210

Currency: Trinidad and Tobago dollar

Time zone: GMT -5

Electricity: 115V 60Hz

Weights and measures: Metric

Religions: Roman Catholic, Hindu, Anglican

Language: English (official), Hindi, French, Spanish, Chinese

Government type: Parliamentary democracy

International dialling code: 00 1 868

National holiday: 31 August, Independence Day

but also through the influence of their various former colonial powers: British, French, Dutch, Danes and Americans. Late twentieth- and early twenty-first-century building is ubiquitous.

Stir into the pot architectural styles from the population majority descended from African slaves, then add contemporary lifestyle ingredients such as golf, tennis, diving and sailing, and you are spoilt for choice. Most islands boast a wide range of properties, including luxury villas, condominiums, townhouses, seafront apartments and plantation or farmhouses inland. At one end of the scale there are luxury properties worth millions of pounds; at the other, there are chattel homes or popular houses, of the type once lived in by slave labour and still highly affordable today.

The one feature they have in common is an emphasis on outdoor living in the hot climate. Houses have a profusion of verandas, porches, galleries, terraces and balconies where so much of daily life takes place. Awash with pots of lush vegetation, they are often a halfway stage between house and garden. The humblest of Caribbean homes tend to have some sort of garden, however small, which constitutes an alfresco living room as lovingly cared for as anything indoors. These gardens provide not only shade, but also plants for food, drink and medicine.

Each island is unique, with its own take on Caribbean real estate, whether style or price. Here is a taste of what you can expect to find on some of those islands in the sun.

types of property

Despite the invasion of concrete and steel, which are necessary imports on those islands lacking in indigenous building materials, some traditional architectural styles can be found throughout the islands, either original or a modern adaptation. The picturesque wooden chattel house in its various forms – the subject of so many Caribbean postcards – is the most obvious example.

These plantation workers' houses (moveable property – as in 'goods and chattels') were the original mobile home as long ago as the eighteenth century. Constructed from prefabricated parts, and sitting on loose foundations, they could be dismantled and rebuilt in new locations dictated by the job market.

Originally made out of leftover wood in natural colours, these two-room houses became highly decorated with the widespread advent of paint between the two world wars. Distinctive features are steeply pitched corrugated iron roofs and jalousie shutters, for ventilation as well as to lessen the impact of hurricanes; and a cool veranda or porch, with gingerbread fretwork to provide shade and shelter from sun and rain. Modern 'off-the-shelf' versions are marketed today on some islands where building land is more readily available.

These workers' cabins were originally dotted around sugar cane plantations. The actual plantation houses themselves, sited at the centre of the estate on high land to take advantage of cooling breezes, are desirable but pricey properties today. Built mainly of wood, with tile roofs, these predominantly one-storey buildings have been enlarged over the years, often with galleries and verandas as well as indoor kitchens and bathrooms.

Barbados, rich in chattel and plantation houses, and every other kind of sunshine architecture, is a long-standing favourite among overseas buyers, especially the British. Compared with most other Caribbean destinations, it is an expensive island where it is possible to spend £1,000,000, and considerably more, to turn the dream of a tropical paradise into reality, especially on the sheltered west coast. However, Bajan luxury is becoming steadily more affordable for those with more modest budgets. And paying that little bit extra for a second home in Barbados means buying into a real estate infrastructure used to dealing with clients from abroad.

It is quite feasible to find traditional two or three-bedroom wooden houses on the beach, but today's overseas buyers increasingly favour new properties. Although Barbados is small, with limited room for residential expansion, the authorities are planning for almost 1,000 new homes in the final half of this decade, many of them in safe gated communities inland but still within striking distance of the coast.

In keeping with international trends, many of them are one or two-bedroom apartments or larger townhouses in so-called lifestyle developments. These communities share facilities such as a swimming pool, tennis courts and sometimes a gym, and sit alongside a golf course or marina. For example, British leisure supremo David Lloyd recently built a complex at Sugar Hill with forty 'tennis apartments' plus courtyard villas, all sharing pool, clubhouse and restaurant.

Another popular former British colony, but not so expensive, is **Antigua**. Almost half its 70,000 population are incomers, many of them Americans arriving since the island's building boom began in the 1980s. They pushed up prices, which dropped after 11 September 2001, but are rising again. Britons are now in the vanguard of prospective homeowners, attracted by properties which tend to be cheaper than in comparable European locations. Most opt to live on or near the coast, rather than in the less attractive interior.

Sure, you can live in £1,000,000 homes in the Jumby Bay Club and Mill Reef areas, or join the golfers at Cedar Valley Golf Club and Jolly Harbour, or boaties at Falmouth or English Harbour, but there are

The Dominican capital of Roseau boasts a number of pretty historic buildings among the town's recent redevelopment.

Jolly Harbour is the largest
marina, golf and beach resort in
the Caribbean. Developed by a
Swiss entrepreneur, Dr Alfred
Erhart, it offers plenty of
opportunities for the overseas
buyer.

waterfront properties at a tenth of the price. And there are basic, small, wooden chattel-style houses at bargain-basement prices. Thanks to the Antiguan Government's policy of affordable homes on affordable freehold land, several companies compete to build these one-, two- or three-bedroom properties.

Mid-range, there is wide choice of property around the £150,000 mark, including two- or three-bedroom waterfront townhouses and countryside Caribbean-style homes with pools. Building your own home is not unusual, with location, view, amenities and services determining the price of land. Typically, a £160,000 cost splits up into £45,000 for the land and the balance for landscaping and building the house and pool.

Dominica, another former British colony, is not the first island that springs to mind among Caribbean homehunters. Its wild coastline provides rare opportunities for oceanfront housing development in a traditional seaside setting, and its few beaches are black volcanic sand. Its 300 square miles of interior are mainly rainforest, rivers and mountains. However, it is just this rugged individuality that attracts the independent get-away-from-it-all type who enjoys living close to nature.

Not being a Caribbean property hotspot, you'd expect relatively cheap prices. But this is offset by a scarcity of building land and materials. Traditional housing, passed down from one generation to the next, rarely goes on the market, so a popular trend among overseas buyers is to purchase a plot of land and build on it. When buying cheap unregistered land, it is essential to have a local solicitor to investigate title to avoid disputes over ownership.

There is land for sale from about one pound a square foot and houses from about £70,000 up to £200,000. People mostly sell because they have fallen on hard times so the properties usually need a lot of work to bring them up to standard. Sometimes it is easier to build exactly what you want.

A solution is to buy a plot on established developments, such as Wallhouse and Belfast on the west coast where services such as roads, water and electricity are in place, then build your own house either to an off-the-peg design or tailor-made by an architect. More upmarket is the Bamboo River development, five minutes from the capital, which has paved roads, street lighting and underground utilities. Expect to pay £20,000 for a plot, and at least three times as much again to build a three-bedroom house.

On **Guadeloupe** and **Martinique** there are advantages and disadvantages for Britons seeking a home. The islands are difficult to get to, the cost of living is pricey and the official language is French – but there are few British and American buyers who tend to drive the Caribbean property market and push up prices. So, like for like, you'd tend to get a better deal here than Barbados, for example, without compromising on quality.

The Gallic influence can be seen in old plantation houses, built in the style of French manor houses or farmhouses. But they are rare. Chic modern properties are more desirable, for those who can afford them, while traditional Caribbean-style houses are less fashionable, and therefore cheaper, especially away from the coast. A price range of £100,000–£150,000 offers a wide choice of properties on either island, with Martinique tending to be the more expensive of the two. For that price, you could find two- and three-bedroom houses, usually with a garden, often with an income-generating self-contained apartment, and sometimes with a pool.

Britons, too, are few and far between among Americans in the US territory of **St Croix**, where you can buy everything from bargain-basement condominiums to family homes in gated communities. The Danish architecture of the harbour towns of Christiansted and Frederiksted are reminders of the past, but modern housing developments are the order of the day, many of them along the Northern Shores near the best golf course. Condos are popular, but association fees can be as high as £500 a month, including hurricane insurance. Property prices tumbled when Hurricane Hugo hit in 1989, but have recovered in recent years.

The cities and towns of **Puerto Rico** are living museums of four centuries of Spanish colonial rule, but Americans, who took over in the late nineteenth century, put their stamp on the island today. Many own second homes there, often modern houses, especially bungalows, which sit alongside traditional colonial houses. Gated communities with 24-hour security proliferate, as do apartment blocks in Spanish costa style. Efficient, safe, cheap – but not necessarily pretty. The touristy east coast has a thriving property market, while the west coast is relatively unspoilt and underdeveloped – and 30 per cent cheaper. Not bad, considering that pricewise Puerto Rico as a whole compares well with other Caribbean islands.

The Caribbean is no longer for the super-rich. Shop around, perhaps considering a less obvious destination such as **Trinidad** where, even though prices

websites

www.fco.gov.uk – information on UK health agreements with other EEA countries

www.caribbean-direct.com – for information about getting around, local services and accommodation in Guadeloupe and Martinique (soon to cover more Caribbean islands)

www.welcometothe caribbean.com – general information about culture, lifestyle, government and economy

www.britishcaribbean. com – information about the High Commissions for the Caribbean in London

have doubled in four years, it is possible to buy a small family home in a safe area for £120,000. Or **Montserrat**, where property prices tumbled after the Soufrière Hills volcano erupted in 1995 but once again attracts 'snowbird' second homeowners who buy to escape cold northern winters.

points to consider

While each island is unique, there have been many recent attempts to form a united Caribbean community with common economic and financial policies and legal systems. This has not happened yet, a fact which has implications for the housebuyer from abroad. In terms of property prices, comparing like with like on different islands is a fruitless exercise without taking many other factors into account – such as acquisition costs and legal fees (dealt with elsewhere).

Note: most Caribbean property is priced in US dollars. Earlier this year (2004) the US currency had weakened against the £ sterling by almost 20 per cent over the previous six months – representing either a considerable saving on the purchase price, or buying that swimming pool or extra bedroom. Of course, advantageous exchange rates attract more buyers, putting pressure on property prices. Remember the old saying about swings and roundabouts. But catch the market at the right time and the sterling holder can find bargains.

The Caribbean is rich in variety and price. House values throughout the region were affected to one extent or another by 9/11, but are bouncing back. Here is just a taste – a rough guide of what is available, bearing in mind that exchange rates and property prices change from one week to the next.

price bands

£25,000–£50,000
- simple chattel house excluding land cost, Antigua
- half-acre building plot, e.g. Domenica or St Croix
- properties needing extensive renovation

£50,000–£100,000
- building cost of two-bed house excluding land, many islands
- family 'live onboard' yacht
- simple two-bed house on many islands, e.g. Trinidad
- small studio apartments/condos in large developments

£100,000–£150,000
- wide range of affordable property on most islands
- villas, townhouses, condos etc.
- four-bed stilted house, Antigua, sea view
- four-bed house in two acres, St Croix rainforest
- three-bed Creole-style house, Martinique
- two-bed Bahamas apartment near beach

£150,000–£200,000

- four-bed beach house on Barbados 'cheap' east coast
- two-bed condos in lifestyle village (e.g. golf, tennis)
- three-bed bungalow, plus pool, some islands, e.g. Tobago
- four-bed houses, most islands, some with self-contained apartments

£200,000–£250,000

- as above, but good location, verandas, balconies etc., self-contained apartments, security, pool, garage, large gardens, luxury imported items (e.g. kitchen fittings, tiles, pool furniture)

£250,000–£500,000

- as above, with extra bedrooms, extensive 'outdoor living', lots of security, and in sought-after locations throughout the Caribbean, e.g. Barbados west coast, Abaco (Bahamas), Jumby Bay Club (Antigua)
- lifestyle living, e.g. two-bed villa on Barbados golf course

£500,000+

- luxury beachfront properties or extensive country estates in prime locations, plus extras such as staff quarters, garages, top-of-the-range security etc.

Les Saintes are a small group of rocky islands five miles to the south of Guadeloupe where life maintains its traditional pace.

Buying property in the Caribbean Q&A

The Caribbean way of life naturally varies from island to island depending on its history and topography. If you are considering buying property there, of course you should do your own individual island research to establish whether or not it is a place where you will be happy. If you can rent a place first, to establish whether or not it's the right place for you, so much the better. To illustrate some of the different possibilities, this introduction to buying property and living in the Caribbean will focus principally on three very different islands: Guadeloupe (and Martinique), St Croix (and the US Virgin Islands) and Antigua.

Q How do I find an estate agent?

A As with almost everywhere in the world, the fastest way of browsing properties and exploring the market is to go online. Otherwise, international property magazines, some property fairs and national newspapers can help although, ultimately, there's no substitute for going to the island and seeing for yourself. Check whether or not there is a licensing procedure for agents. For instance, in Guadeloupe and Martinique, agents are licensed as they are in France and should have a *carte professionelle*. Always check whether or not they belong to a professional body such as FNAIM (Fédération Nationale d'Immobilier) or, in the case of the Virgin Islands, the National Association of Realtors, or one of the other similar organizations that should give you some protection. Also ask for their insurance details. If, as in Antigua for instance, there is no such licensing procedure and almost anyone can hang out an estate agent sign, you are advised to use solicitors as the escrow agent (i.e. to retain the deposit in a third-party account) and to check all legal aspects of the transaction.

Q Is the procedure for buying property the same on every island?

A Given the history of the different islands, they each have their own variations. However the same principles exist.

Q Can a non-resident buy property on any of the islands?

A The rules concerning the acquisition of property vary from island to island. There are no restrictions on Barbados, although formal permission must be granted by the Central Bank of Barbados. In many islands such as St Lucia and Grenada, Dominica and Antigua foreign buyers have to obtain an Alien Landholder's Licence that costs a percentage of the purchase price of the property and takes some months to get through. Since Guadeloupe and Martinique are part of France and therefore of the EU, there are no restrictions on British buyers. The US Virgin Islands and Puerto Rico follow US immigration laws.

Q Are there any other strings attached?

A Because of island variations, you will need to go into the fine detail with your solicitor. For example, on Antigua a solicitor must be retained to apply for the permit from the Ministry of Agriculture and Land and the application must be approved by the Cabinet. Two conditions must be fulfilled: police clearance from the country you come from and evidence of sufficient funds. They may also ask for a bank reference and character references.

Q What happens once I've found a property I like?

A Again, it depends on the island. You will be guided by your estate agent but always consult a solicitor.

In Guadeloupe and Martinique, the French system of purchase is followed with variances that include incentives to buy property and more relaxed rules

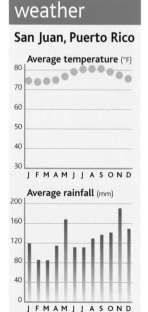

weather

San Juan, Puerto Rico

Average temperature (°F)

80
70
60
50
40
30

J F M A M J J A S O N D

Average rainfall (mm)

200
160
120
80
40
0

J F M A M J J A S O N D

than the homeland when it comes to planning and building. Important to remember are the French inheritance laws which differ from those in the UK. Advice should be taken as to the ways of accommodating them. The buyer is allowed a seven-day cooling off period but this should be specified in the *Compromis de Vente* with the other conditional clauses. After signature, the *notaire* will get the equivalent of a Land Registry search from the *Conservation des Hypotheques* plus a *Note* or *Certificat d'Urbanisme* from the local authority declaring existing uses of land, administrative restrictions that apply and other details of development. Property inspection is not mandatory although it is worth it in case structural problems occur later. On signature of the *Acte de Vente* in the presence of a *notaire*, it is forwarded to the Foreign and Commonwealth Office where a certificate, *l'Apostille*, gives legal effect. The process usually takes three to four months.

Not surprisingly, the US Virgin Islands and Puerto Rico follow the US system (see USA, p. 65), with the whole procedure from presenting your offer and 10 per cent deposit to completion of contract usually taking approximately two months. Otherwise many of the islands follow the British model of purchase with variations. For example, in Barbados, the purchaser will require a registered Barbadian attorney to search the register and establish title to the property prior to the completion of sale to ensure that there are no impediments to the sale. It normally takes two to three months for all the legal issues to be resolved.

If buying on a development, different fees, processes and payments may apply depending on the developer.

Once clustered round its harbour, Martinique's capital Fort-de-France has expanded into the narrow streets that climb into the hills behind.

Q What additional costs am I likely to find?

A Most islands levy duty and/or property transfer tax (usually between 5 and 10 per cent although in Antigua the purchaser only pays 2 per cent of the value of the land, which tends to be assessed as the purchase price). There are also legal fees and extraordinary fees for alien landholder's licence (e.g. 10 per cent in Dominica or 5 per cent in Antigua plus an application fee although in Jolly Harbour and other developments, it may be reduced to 3 per cent for first-time buyers). There may be property taxes to be paid annually, but in Antigua these are negligible. If you plan to rent your property, consider the associated

costs covering the upkeep of the property, its management and rental commission. If your property is part of a larger resort development, there may be community charges to pay, in which case, make sure you know what they cover.

Q What other considerations should I make when buying property?

A If buying land or planning renovations, make sure you are going to be able to get planning permission before you sign any contract. When insuring your property, remember on the relevant islands to cover it for hurricane and earthquake damage.

Q Do I need a visa?

A It depends on the island.

In the French Antilles, UK residents do not need a visa. If visiting for less than six months, all that's needed is a passport and a return or ongoing ticket. A resident's permit may be required although they are no longer necessary in mainland France. Apply to the local prefecture.

Fustic House in Barbados is an old colonial coral brick house designed by theatre designer, Oliver Messel. It lies in the undulating pasturelands and sugar cane fields of the St Lucy Coast.

Entry requirements to the US Virgin Islands and Puerto Rico are the same as for the USA (see USA, p. 69).

A visit of less than six months to Antigua demands a passport, return/ongoing ticket, confirmation of accommodation and evidence of sufficient financial support. A permanent residence scheme was introduced in 1995 to encourage a limited number to establish tax residency there. An application for permanent residence requires the ownership of property on the island, an Alien Landholding Licence, a purchaser's stamp duty, an annual levy of US$20,000 per year and residence on the island for more than thirty days a year.

Living in the Caribbean

government and economy

Guadeloupe is an Overseas Department of France divided into thirty-four communes and thirty-six cantons. As such it is part of the EEC and French law applies. A Prefect appointed by the French Minister of the Interior is assisted by two General Secretaries and two Sous-Préfets. The island has two legislative bodies both locally elected: the Conseil Général and the Conseil Régional. The islanders also elect two representatives to the French Senate, four to the French

National Assembly and two to the Economic Council.

The economy depends on agriculture, tourism and light industry as well as subsidies and imports from France.

The American Virgin Islands are an organized, unincorporated territory of the US with policy regulations under the jurisdiction of the Office of Insular Affairs, US Department of the Interior. Most US Federal laws, rules and regulations apply to the islands. Every two years, a representative is elected to the US House of Representatives. There are no representatives in the Senate. A governor of the islands is elected every four years with a fifteen-member unicameral legislature elected every two years. Judicial power is vested in VI Territorial Court and District Court under the third circuit in the federal Court System.

Tourism (accounting for 70 per cent of the GDP and 70 per cent of employment) is the main economic activity although there is a manufacturing sector that includes petrol refining, textiles, electronics, pharmaceuticals and watch assembly.

Antigua and **Barbuda** were once part of the British Commonwealth and are still part of the Commonwealth of Nations. The Antiguan government reflects this in that it has a UK-style bi-cameral Parliament. Seventeen members of the House of representatives are elected by popular vote while seventeen members of the Senate are appointed by the Governor, mainly on the advice of the Prime Minister and the Leader of the Opposition. The Prime Minister conducts affairs with his cabinet appointed by the Governor General and together they are responsible to the Parliament.

Tourism (50 per cent of the GDP) dominates the economy. Agricultural production mainly supplies domestic needs and is limited by lack of water and the lure of higher wages in tourism and industry.

education

The system of education on **Guadeloupe** and **Martinique** is distinctly French and offers just as high standards in both private and state schools with languages a core part of the curriculum. Schooling is compulsory between six and sixteen, dividing into: Ecole Primaire (primary school) from six to eleven; Collège (lower secondary) where students complete the certificate, Brévat des Collèges; Lycée d'Ensignement général et téchnologique (upper secondary) where they earn the Baccalauréat général or Baccalauréat technologique. The language of instruction is French. Private schools are usually Catholic, fee-based with teachers often from mainland France on short contracts.

St Croix offers both state-funded and private schools providing education from nursery care to the University of the Virgin Islands. Compulsory education follows American lines (see USA, p. 72) culminating in the award of a high school diploma.

The education system in **Antigua** and **Barbuda** follows the British pattern, including both state and private schools with private schools having their own final qualifying examinations and state schools using a standard test. In secondary education, students take the Caribbean Examination Council exams or Cambridge

weather

Camp Jacob, Guadeloupe

Average temperature (°F)

Average rainfall (mm)

University exams or 'O' levels. Some students go on to take 'A' levels to qualify for entry to the regional University of the West Indies or to foreign universities.

health care

Most islands in the Caribbean do not have any sort of healthcare agreement with the UK. Residents from the UK with holiday homes are strongly advised to take out comprehensive medical insurance to secure medical care. In an emergency, you may need to be flown to the neighbouring United States, so ensure that your insurance provides for that.

Both **Guadeloupe** and **Martinique** boast up to twenty modern hospitals and clinics. There is an air ambulance, diving decompression chamber, emergency dental facilities, pharmaceutical services and a twenty-four-hour A&E department available. Since the islands are part of the EEA, an E111 (available from the Post Office) provides free basic health care cover; however, taking out private insurance is a wise precaution nonetheless.

In **La Croix**, as the USA, there is no state-funded medical coverage. Treatment by a doctor or in hospital can be expensive so, again, private health insurance is recommended for residents and non-residents alike.

Antigua has several GPs and specialists, a hospital and a private clinic. Access to health care for residents is through mandatory participation in the Medical Benefits Scheme although supplemental health insurance is recommended.

pensions

Again, advice should be sought before moving to accommodate the different positions taken by the islands. Retirees will be able to continue receiving their pension with the annual increments. See www.dwp.gov.uk.

pets

Most islands don't quarantine imported animals but you will need an Official Certificate of Veterinary Inspection from a government approved vet (LVI). All dogs are subject to local vaccination requirements which you should check before moving. Some islands, e.g. Antigua may demand you apply for an import permit (visit www.antigua-barbuda.org for more information).

If planning on returning the animal to the UK, check whether the island is on the UK Pet Travel Scheme (PETS) which requires you to apply for a pet passport (see USA: Pets, p. 73). If not, visit www.defra.gov.uk for more information.

driving

Which side of the road you drive on in the Caribbean depends on the island and naturally driving conditions depend on the topography, some with steep windy roads, and the care taken to maintain the roads. Martinique and Guadeloupe drive on the right (with Puerto Rico and the Dutch Antilles) whereas Antigua and St Croix drive on the left with the rest. The US Virgin Islands are the only US possession to

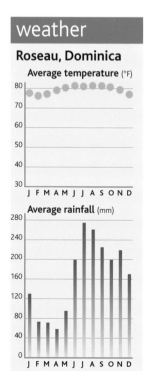

weather

Roseau, Dominica

Average temperature (°F)

Average rainfall (mm)

drive on the left, though the cars are left-hand drive which can make overtaking more of a hazard. Guadeloupe and Martinique require the possession of an International Driving Licence. Roads are well maintained and include some major six-lane highways. If moving to St Croix, you have four months in which to surrender your driving licence and get a US Virgin Islands licence. All main roads are tarmaced with dirt side roads and have a speed limit of 25–35mph. In Antigua, major roads are usually in good condition. Vehicles often lack working safety and signalling devices and traffic regulations are not always rigidly enforced. To drive here, you need an international driver's licence and a permit to drive in Antigua. The permit is valid for three months. It can be extended twice and then the holder is eligible for a permanent Antiguan licence.

Harbour Island's Dunmore Town is one of the Bahamas most charming settlements with its colonial houses and white picket fencing.

car

If you want to take your car to an island, you will have to investigate their particular importation regulations. The cost of shipping and registering it may well not make it worthwhile.

taxes

Many Caribbean islands do not levy income tax and where they do it is relatively low compared to the UK. British retirees may not be liable to pay tax on income earned abroad. Few islands charge capital gains tax. In the French Antilles, the French tax regime applies with a PAYE system for residents that is, however, cheaper than on the French mainland. In the US Virgin Islands, the US federal rules apply (www.irs.gov). In Antigua, individuals are not subject to income tax whereas in Dominica the personal allowance is EC15,000 with tax rates rising from 20 per cent to 40 per cent depending on income.

Obtain expert financial advice before you move or buy a holiday home that you plan to rent. The implications may differ depending on the island you choose.

House-hunters

Martinique
James and Christine Pearson
Budget: £150,000

Renovating their home in Tonbridge, Kent, meant that Christine and James Pearson could realistically consider selling up and being able to afford a permanent home in the Caribbean where they had spent many holidays. They had returned time after time, having fallen in love with the lifestyle, the weather, the inviting sea and the views. Christine's ambition was to give up her work in a local shopping centre to relax by the beach while James, a former shipwright in the navy, loves water sports and was looking forward to a more active life.

Le Diamant. Three-bedroom Caribbean house with living room, kitchen, two shower rooms and veranda; self-contained ground-floor studio apartment; garden, plunge pool with decking area: £150,000.

They started their search in the south of the island in **Le Diamant**, 'the diamond'. Named after the imposing rock just off the shore where, in 1804, the French are believed to have tricked the British army encamped on the rock. They floated out barrels of rum to them so that the next morning, they could easily capture them while sleeping off the after-effects. Just at the edge of the resort was a modern Caribbean house painted in traditional Caribbean colours of yellows and aqua blues and greens. The Pearsons entered via the kitchen and were immediately struck by the wonderful view. The kitchen itself had tiled splashbacks and vividly painted shutters and doors with fitted wooden units. The living room with one bright yellow wall was small with a floor tiled to resemble a carpet and surround. The airy master bedroom was a good size but had no built-in storage. Downstairs, the studio apartment had generous dimensions and included a neat kitchen. It was the ideal solution for visiting friends and family who could cater for themselves. If the Pearsons decided to let it, it was estimated that they should be able to get between £250 and £300 per week during the peak months. As for the pool, it was small enough for Christine to be able to swim 100 lengths! But it did boast a view to St Lucia. This was exactly the sort of property the couple were hoping to see although ultimately they felt it was more of a holiday home than they were after and the colours might be a bit much in the long term.

Next on the agenda was a retreat high above the quiet fishing village of **Petite Anse**. Most of the houses in the area are owned by fishermen and very little comes on the open market so this was a rare find. It was something of a hike to get up the hill to the property but once there, the views over the bay were simply breathtaking. A long veranda ran outside the house that had a large cool tiled living room with views to both sides and a through breeze. The kitchen and breakfast bar were dated and needed modernizing. Being able to see through the house gave an illusion of greater space. The blue master bedroom was a good size though it had no

fitted cupboards. Outside, the circular pool was draped with bougainvillea. The most off-putting feature was the steep climb to the house, The concrete drive was the responsibility of the owners of the house and, to avoid it becoming slippery in a downpour, needed resurfacing at an approximate cost of £3,000. Although bowled over by the views, the Pearsons agreed that the property presented too many dangers for their grandchildren and they would have to fence it in. And then there was the climb …

Above: Petite Anse. Two-bedroom retreat with kitchen, living room and pantry; separate studio apartment and bathroom; secluded garden with seating area circular pool: £140,000.

They continued their search in **St Anne**, a busy town that has retained its 1940s charm but is now considered Martinique's watersports capital. Built only two years ago the modern colonial-style house was large for its price tag but it did need some work. The kitchen was basic but came with fitted wooden units and a gas hob. The living/dining room was spacious and tiled throughout to keep it cool. The two bedrooms were huge (the second bedroom contained three double beds!) The large veranda from the master bedroom had an area that was used as a gym. There were two further large verandas on the ground floor, one overlooking the pool and garden and another running the entire length along the side of the house. The current owner had done a rather makeshift conversion of the basement so the washing machine had been eccentrically located on the veranda. However, James

Below: St Anne. Three-bedroom beach house with kitchen, open-plan living/dining room, bathroom and huge basement; garden, patio, barbecue area and pool: £150,000.

and Christine thought that the idea of stripping the basement out to provide a blank canvas on which they could start from scratch was a good one. The space had the potential for conversion to either a separate apartment or an additional four bedrooms. But renovation work was hardly the reason they wanted to move to the Caribbean so they decided against the place.

Finally they headed inland to the rainforest around **St Luce** where a stunning luxury villa offered all they asked as well as having considerable earning potential. The light, airy living room had high-beamed ceilings and a soothing through breeze that blew through the arched doors and

St Luce. Two-bedroom luxury villa with living/dining room, kitchen, bathroom and large mezzanine area; four separate studio apartments; garden: £186,000.

windows. The current owners had made the most of the space using comfortable low-slung cream sofas and chairs. The contemporary kitchen had plenty of units and wall cupboards that the Pearsons appreciated. The master bedroom had a very large en suite bathroom with marble steps leading up to a marble double bath and a dressing room area. The second bedroom had a large shower room with a double-size shower. All four of the self-contained apartments had a compact fitted kitchen, living area, bedroom area, large fully tiled shower room and patio area. They were ready for occupation, potentially bringing in £250 per week each during both peak seasons. If they decided to put them in the hands of a French lettings agency, they could expect to pay the agency about £50 per week, leaving them with a maximum income of £21,000 per year. James and Christine were extremely excited about the property, thinking that it was 'huge, well-decorated and with lots of room for their visiting family'. The only snag was the lack of a pool but that could be rectified with the acquisition of an adjacent piece of land and besides, they were only ten minutes from the beach.

When they returned to England they made the decision that they would try to buy both the house in St Anne and the St Luce house. They planned to reconvert the basement in the St Anne house which would have had its own private entrance, garden and parking and updated the main house. This property would hopefully have been their main source of rental income supplemented by any lettings from the four apartments. In fact, a family illness made James and Christine rethink their priorities, realizing that they wanted to have easier and quicker access to the UK than Martinique would give them. In the future, they will continue to holiday there.

House-hunters

Antigua

Mark and Debbie Anderson
Budget: £130,000

Exotic holidays are one way to discover where on earth you would like to be for a little longer. As a result of theirs, Debbie and Mark Anderson had got married four years earlier in the Caribbean and had now decided to invest in a second home there. They loved the scenery, the beaches and the sea and were so determined to buy a holiday home there that they were prepared to sacrifice space to be by the sea, aware that property here can be expensive. This was the first time they'd visited

Antigua but were excited by what they'd heard.

The first property they saw was on the north-west of the island in one of the biggest resorts – **Dickenson Bay**. It was an ideal location for Mark and Debbie because they wanted a property with good rental potential; their 17-year-old son Mark liked action holidays and they wanted the scenery to go with it. Inside, the villa was light, bright and white, the floors tiled throughout. In the living room, the owners had used white garden furniture which increased the sense of merging indoors and outdoors, as well as giving a feeling of space. The small kitchen area was newly done and Debbie was particularly taken by the hand-painted Caribbean tiles. The master bedroom was cool and restful with fabulous views and an en suite bathroom finished with mosaic tiles. The guest bedroom had its own separate entrance and veranda and was so large that it would be ideal as a separate bedsit for their son or to rent. The holiday season runs from 1 December to 1 May and the Andersons could expect to receive a rental income of about £640 per week, totalling £12,000 per year. They were both impressed with the place, commenting on the space afforded by the high ceilings and the fact that every room offered a staggering view.

Above: Dickenson Bay. Two-bedroom villa with living/dining room, kitchen, two shower rooms; veranda and patio garden: £106,000.

Next they headed towards the southern resorts, beyond the Shekerley mountains to the little town of **Jolly Harbour**. Built along one of the best beaches on the island, the town was built specifically to attract foreign investors. The marina is the largest in the Caribbean and smart villas with their own moorings appeal to affluent holidaymakers from Europe and America. There was a private complex close to the quayside where Mark and Debbie could see a show home with a view to buying a small two-bedroom house. The kitchen was smart and painted in neutral tones, large enough to contain a big fridge-freezer. The living room was a decent size and gave onto a veranda with more sensational views across the water. The master bedroom was big enough to contain a four-poster bed and benefited from the light pouring in through the patio doors. The second room was painted a very Caribbean yellow and had great fitted wardrobes. There was easy access to both the Olympic-sized pool or one mile of white sandy beach but the real drawcard was the outside veranda and the steps down to the water. Debbie thought waterfront living was the height of chic and was prepared to consider the possibility of one day paying an additional £3,600 for a mooring. Without the terrace, the house would cost £98,000 plus any of the optional extras. A glamorous possibility but too big for the Andersons.

Below: Jolly Harbour. Two-bedroom quayside home with two bathrooms, living/dining room, breakfast balcony and access to the waterway; buggy garage; communal pool, tennis courts, golf club: £101,000.

Jabberwock Bay, on the east coast of the island, has always appealed to the younger set. There are few holiday homes on this part of the island and very little for sale but Mark and Debbie were lucky enough

Above: Jabberwock Bay. Currently a small office; originally a three-bedroom house with living room, three shower rooms, a storeroom and kitchen; veranda and garden: £119,000.

to find a traditional Antiguan house with bags of potential. The original living area was being used as a large open-plan office but could be reconverted into a living/dining area again. The dark oak floors had been waxed and polished and the original windows looked out over the garden. A hatch leads through to the kitchen that needed some modernizing but it did have fitted units and a large storeroom that could be used as a pantry. All three bedrooms were on the same floor and all being used as office space. The original master bedroom was the manager's deluxe office. It had windows along two walls, air-conditioning and an en suite shower room decorated with the original tile. Outside a large veranda added character to the house, and a pretty garden was big enough for a swimming pool. The privacy of the garden would be enhanced with the addition of a fast-growing hedge at the back while the cost of the pool would be as much as £20,000. However, despite the massive rooms, the Andersons felt they needed to remember the rental potential of whatever they bought and, because of its location, its appeal would be limited.

Finally they travelled to **St John's**, the capital of the island. The town is packed with souvenir stalls and markets but is famous for the duty-free designer boutiques found in the old molasses warehouses on the waterfront. As everywhere on the island, the beaches by St John's are spectacular but, because there are fewer package holiday companies operating here, they tend to be quieter than other areas. There was a brand new complex right by the beach that had only just begun to be marketed. Nine out of the thirty-two properties were so far under offer. Once an old timeshare complex built twelve years ago, it had been transformed into a gated community with a rather exclusive feel. All that remained was for the restaurant to be completed and the beach to be spruced up. The house was painted yellow with white woodwork and verandas. Inside, the cool aquamarine living room was extremely stylish, big patio doors leading to a terrace with stunning views. It wasn't hard for Mark and Debbie to imagine sunning themselves there all day. The kitchen was perfectly fitted and an ideal size while the master bedroom was so big, it currently housed two double beds. The house definitely represented good value for money and Debbie was blown away by it, despite Mark's reservations. An added attraction was its position only a twenty-minute drive from the airport with a potential rental of £750 during the high season.

Below: St John's. Three-bedroom house with living room, dining room, bathroom, kitchen; veranda: £125,000.

Mark's own favourite was the clifftop villa. It sold itself to him on the strength of its views and for him stood out above the others although Debbie felt it

was a little too precarious for her liking. They decided to revisit the two favourites to see if one shone through. Mark persuaded Debbie that the clifftop villa was the one for them. After consulting their financial adviser, they instructed a local surveyor to look at the villa. Unfortunately he reported some subsidence, so after some consideration, the Andersons decided not to go further. Instead, having in the meantime visited a property show at Earls Court, they flew to Newfoundland where they bought a one and a half acre plot in the Humber Valley Resort and are building their own house there, due for completion in August 2004.

House-hunters

Puerto Rico

Pegy Gaile and Mel Waldron
Budget: £75,000

Friends since they were five years old, singer-songwriter and fashion designer Pegy Gaile and her best friend Mel Waldron, mother of two from Derby, both have Caribbean parents and were keen to get back to their roots by buying a holiday home in Puerto Rico. Depending on what they found, they thought they might buy separately or pool resources if it meant getting a better bargain. Bearing in mind their budget, they concentrated their search on the undeveloped west coast where property prices were around 33 per cent lower than the rest of the island.

The first port of call was **Rincón**, popular with surfers and host to major international surfing competitions. The atmosphere of the town is relaxed retro and young Puerto Ricans and American surfers buy or rent second homes in the area. As elsewhere in the Caribbean, properties tend to be geared towards a tropical outdoors lifestyle and the one they viewed was no exception. From the outside, this semi-detached house presented a bright Caribbean face to the world with its painted walls and intricate wrought-iron work. A terracotta-tiled floor unified the interior from the comfortable living room with its cream walls and wicker furniture, through the modern kitchen with white units, ceiling fan and room for a sofa, to the breakfast room, surrounded by windows overlooking the garden. The overall impression was one of space and light. Sunshine also flooded into the long narrow master bedroom that, with the other two bedrooms, benefited from renovated bathrooms. The self-contained apartment on the ground floor could be rented but would also make a great space for the kids. Outside the terrace was large enough for entertaining and currently sported a pool table. The two women thought the garden below would make a fine vegetable plot. Both of them liked the area, quiet and safe for kids, but ultimately felt the layout of the house was too 'messy'.

Below: Rincón. Three-bedroom semi-detached house with bathroom, kitchen, living room, breakfast room and dining room; Self-contained apartment; terrace and garden: £76,000.

It was on to the breathtaking surroundings of the **Combate National Park**. Although the west of the island is the driest part, the landscape here is lush thanks to the trade winds fanning the coast. The salt reserves have made the region an important area in the island's history but now it is more famous as a breeding area for the Puerto Rican horses used in rodeos. It was here that Mel and Pegy saw an attractive wooden house with loads of character. Inside, the main entrance led straight into the open-plan living/dining area and kitchen. The natural timber walls were left exposed and high ceilings and large windows contributed to an impressive sense of space and light. The master bedroom with en suite bathroom

Above: Combate National Park. Two-bedroom house with open-plan living/dining room, kitchen and bathroom; self-contained apartment; workshop and garden: £75,000.

was warm and bright with private access to the balcony. The balcony itself spanned the width of the house and had plenty of room for sitting out and admiring the fabulous views across to the sea. The second bedroom was a fair size with enough space to double as a playroom and next door was a shared bathroom. Downstairs a large self-contained apartment was ideal for letting. Currently unfurnished, it had a separate living area and a basic kitchen with gas oven. There was also a large workshop in the garden that was fully plumbed and wired and could make a great self-contained unit. Building permission usually takes about six to eight weeks to come through and the total cost of conversion would probably amount to £2,000. Pegy was particularly taken by this one, loving the wild surroundings and the house's character but the house wasn't large enough for Mel and her family.

Below: Boquerón. Three-bedroom, two bathroom apartment with living room, kitchen, dining room; rooftop terrace; communal swimming pool and basketball court: £120,000.

They continued their search in the fishing village of **Boquerón** where they looked round a show apartment on a new complex. Boquerón is an up-and-coming resort with a safe family-oriented beach protected from dangerous waves and currents by its horseshoe shaped bay. Over the last few years, the modest fishing harbour has burgeoned into a flashy marina popular with affluent businessmen. To buy the apartment, Mel and Pegy would have to pool resources. Would they like it? The living room was decorated in cool shades and had air conditioning plus french windows onto the terraces. The galley kitchen was white and divided from the dining area by an island. The master bedroom was large, airy and simple. Outside the terrace and barbecue area was shaded by judicious planting while the roof terrace provided a wonderful chillout area with views to the sea. Both women loved it, especially the roof terrace, and could envisage great pool parties. They were not put off by the communal charges of £60 per month that covered exterior maintenance of the property, the pool and tennis court. However they were concerned with the idea of community living and being less than ideal neighbours when it came to partying and noise.

Lastly, they travelled to **Ponce**, Puerto Rico's second largest city, to view a luxury villa. Named after Juan Ponce de Leon, the town benefited from the wealth of the sugar cane industries, clearly visible in the architecture of the city. Mel and Pegy visited a quiet upmarket suburb where a luxury villa with a large terrace, outside bar and country-style garden was for sale. The formal living area had been elaborately furnished but it was a generous space and led into a big white modern kitchen. Light reflected off the polished floor tiles of the cool pink master bedroom that had its own balcony. Outside, there was plenty of room for entertaining and partying. Both women loved everything about the property, from the terrace at the front of the house where you could sit and watch the world go by to the huge master bedroom with its en suite bathroom. They felt the whole place presented an elegant

and tranquil face to the world and were particularly interested to learn that because the owner wanted a quick sale he was open to negotiation. It was recommended that, if they were interested, they should make an opening offer of £145,000. As far as they were concerned this was the place for them. All that remained for them to do was to return to England so that Mel could talk to her husband and bring him back to the island to see the property for himself before they committed. However he felt it was too far away so instead Mel will have to look forward to staying with Pegy who is still hoping to find a holiday home for herself.

Above: Ponce. Three-bedroom luxury villa with two bathrooms, kitchen, dining room and living room; terrace with barbecue area an large, picturesque garden: £156,000.

Ex-pat experience

Dominica

Tina Alexander

When Tina Alexander visited with a church group in 1988, the last thing she expected was to fall in love with the rainforest island and its people, not to mention her husband, Harry. To cut a long story short, she ended up exchanging her life as a social worker in East London for the green mountains and rushing rivers of Dominica.

'When we first came to Dominica, it was really a faith venture, we were newly married and neither of us had employment,' she remembers. 'We rented a tiny downstairs apartment and were flooded out with the first tropical storm. I remember faxing our first newsletter home saying that the volcano had erupted and a curfew had been imposed due to rioting taxi drivers and frightening my mother to death! However the volcano has never again been in the news, the riots were short-lived and, with a change of government, the demonstrations soon became unnecessary.'

Within six months Tina had a job as Dominica's only psychiatric social worker and Harry was an assistant minister in the local Pentecostal church. 'Despite being the only white person in the congregation, I was soon accepted as Sister Tina and the church networks continue to be an important part of my life. I worked in my

Above: Tina and Harry's house at purchase and below, now.

job for seven years and drove a green bus very badly all over the island doing community follow-up. Once I drove into a deep drain and had to be pulled by a group of Rastafarians with their bare hands. Who needs the RAC?!'

As Harry is Dominican, Tina had no difficulty with residency and her employer, the Ministry of Health, sorted out her work permit. 'I am now a citizen of Dominica and as I am fond of saying in patois, "Mon ka westay pou bon." Or "I am staying for good."'

They bought a wreck of a house for about £50,000 and spent twice as much converting it into a two-storey building with their three-bedroom home downstairs and a four-bedroom guest apartment and Tina's office upstairs.

With only 70,000 people on the island, the local hospital can only offer basic services although getting a consultant is easy and a GP makes house calls within a few hours of contacting them. 'We have been blessed with good health and my two deliveries were straightforward so we have never needed to go overseas for serious treatment. Martinique is just one hour away on the ferry, faster by air ambulance, so we are not really at any more risk than if we were in a remote part of a large country.' Because Harry is now a public servant, working in the hospital, the family do have a cheap insurance policy so even their doctor's, dentist's and medication bills are covered.

With the arrival of their two children, Ben (5) and Miriam (7), Harry and Tina have become concerned with education. 'We have a small private primary school which is run quite cheaply by the parents – we pay about £300 a term. We have qualified ex-pat teachers and some experienced Dominicans too. The population of the school is very mixed and our children feel quite at home. The same group of parents that started the primary school (Pioneer Prep) are now embarking on a secondary school (Orion Secondary). It was opened last September with fifteen pupils. By the time our children need it I expect it will have expanded considerably. If not, the grammar school and Convent High are OK but the classes are a bit large, the facilities very limited and their range of subjects small.'

It is likely that Miriam and Ben will eventually return to Britain to go to university, although most students go to UWI or the USA as they never forget that they are British as well as Dominican. 'We can get *Fawlty Towers* and *Blackadder* on BBC America, one of fifty plus cable TV channels, so they are being initiated into the British humour of our generation.'

As the years have gone by, Tina and Harry have established an accommodation agency to help people looking for holidays, long-term rentals or homes and land to purchase (see www.islandguests.dm). In 2001 they set up Lifeline Ministries to help small community-based organizations to access funds and complete various projects and training programmes. In Dominica, a small grant goes a long way.

'We have seen two bridges built, six youth training schemes, several projects with disabled people and an educational trust fund established. We also seek sponsors for disabled children as the services here are very limited.' Tina has always enjoyed counselling and is now in her third year of studies towards a Masters with the University of West Indies. 'Our class is made up of eighty-three students across ten territories from Belize to the Bahamas and we link up by tele-conferencing every week. There are five of us here in Dominica and it is so exciting to be involved at the forefront of an emerging profession.'

With so much going on in her life, it seems absurd to ask what she misses from England. 'Leaving friends and family was hard but many of our closest buddies have already visited us and had an adventure here. They stay in touch by collecting whatever people want to donate and sending them to us.' Also on the list of things they miss are sausages and mushrooms, concerts, autumn and winter, the sales, Tesco's, English jokes and fish and chips. But what a lot they have to compensate.

'Dominica is a young country, full of hopes and aspirations, recovering from colonialism and aiming to be very different from its neighbours. We do not have golden beaches or lots of sophisticated tourism technology but we have river-rafting, an aerial tram, rare parrots and humming birds, whales and dolphins and wonderful sunsets over the Caribbean Sea. I am a large fish in a very beautiful small pond, and love it.'

'Leaving friends and family was hard but many of our closest buddies have already visited us and had an adventure here.'

Further Reading

general travel guides

The *Rough Guides* published by The Rough Guides
The *Lonely Planet Guides* published by Lonely Planet Publications
The *Footprint Guides* published by Footprint Handbooks
Eyewitness Travel Guides published by Dorling Kindersley
The *Essential Series* published by AA Books
Globetrotter Guides published by New Holland

Living Abroad by Michael Furnell and Philip Jones, Kogan Page
Buying a Home Abroad by David Hampshire, Survival Books, Ltd

Living and Working in Australia by David Hampshire, Survival Books Ltd
Live and Work in Australia and New Zealand by Dan Boothby and Susan Kelly, Vacation Work Publications
Living and Working in Australia by Laura Veltman, How To Books

Living and Working in America by Steve Mills, How To Books
Living and Working in America by David Hampshire, Survival Books Ltd
Buying a Property in Florida by Christian Moen, John Howell, Cadogan Guides
Live and Work in the USA and Canada by Victoria Pybus, Vacation Work Publications

magazines

Homes Overseas call 020 7939 9888 or visit www.homesoverseas.co.uk for details
World of Property call 01323 726040 or visit www.worldofproperty.co.uk for details
Place in the Sun call 01342 828 700 or visit www.aplaceinthesunmag.co.uk for details
Florida Magazine (bi-monthly UK magazine) visit www.thefloridamagazine.com for details

property exhibitions

Homes Overseas Exhibitions 020 7939 9888 or visit www.homesoverseas.co.uk for details
World of Property call 01323 726040 or visit www.worldofproperty.co.uk for details

Useful Addresses

The publishers and Freeform TV would like to thank the following companies for their help in making the programmes and this book. Please note that Pan Macmillan and Freeform are not endorsing these companies, and it is your own responsibility to ensure that any advice you seek from them comes from a fully qualified professional.

lawyers

Complete Legal Solutions Lawyers Incorporating Conveyancing Solutions and Legal Mortgage Solutions

Level 1
96 Albert St
Brisbane
Qld 4000
Australia
Tel: 07 3229 5576
Fax: 07 3229 4486
Email: dean.farnham@completelegal.com.au
Web: www.completelegal.com.au

McWilliams & Elliott Attorneys

P O Box 45
Port Elizabeth
6001
South Africa
Tel: 041 5821250

Murphy Wallace Slabbert Inc

P O Box 3856
Cape Town
8001
South Africa
Tel: 00 27 (0)21 422 0570
Fax: 00 27 (0)21 422 0913
Email: info@murphys-law.co.za
Web: www.murphys-law.co.za

Richards Anjo & Associates

Victoria Chambers
Old Anjo Insurances Bldg
Lower Long Street
P.O.Box 3575
St. John's
Antigua
Tel: 268-562-1705
Fax: 268-562-1706
E: Mail : richards@candw.ag
Web: www.antigualaw.com

John Howell Solicitors

17 Maiden Lane
Covent Garden
London WC2E 7NL
Tel: 020 7420 0400
Fax: 020 7836 3626
Email: london@legal21.org

estate agents

Eugenie Smith International

Tel: 01425 619132
Fax: 01202 487949
Email: Eugenie@eugeniesmith.com
Web: www.eugeniesmith.com

Australia
New South Wales
First National

Tel: 0061 244 725 566
Web: www.sydneyrealtors.com.au

Marshall & Tacheci

Tel: 0061 264 933 333
Web: www.marshallandtacheci.com.au

Merimbula Lake Real Estate

Tel: 0061 264 951 522

Fairway 17

Tel: 0061 244 722 999
Web: www.southcoast.com.au/fairway17

Perth
Remax Realmark

Tel: 0061 89307 0989
Web: www.realmark.com.au

Lynda Moore

Tel: 0061 89574 0500
Web: www.ljh.com.au

Rundin Realty
Tel: 0061 89295 3222
Web: www.reiwa.com.au

LJ Hooker – Glen Forrest
Tel: 0061 89298 9300
Web: www.ljh.com.au

Jacaranda Coast
Professionals, Maclean
Tel: 0061 266 455 000
Web: www.macleanrealestate.com.au

Bob Hamilton Real Estate
Tel: 0061 411 815 244
Web: www.midcoast.com.au

Moy & Darby Real Estate
Tel: 0061 266 432 455
Web: www.professionals.com.au/moy&darby/

Cardow Webster
Tel: 0061 266 541 148
Web: www.cardowwebster.com.au

Queensland
Cairns Beaches Realty
Tel: 0061 740 577 044
Web: www.cairnsbeachesrealty.com.au

Raine & Horne
Tel: 0061 740 996 900
Web: www.rainehorneqld.com.au

Angela Capitanio Realty
Tel: 0061 740 510 555
Web: www.angelacapitanio.com

USA
Florida's First Coast
Watson Realty
Tel: 001 904 461 9066
Web: www.watsonrealtycorp.com

Century 21 AIA Realty
Tel: 001 904 471 2121
Web: www.century21A1Arealty.com

Realty Executives
Tel: 001 386 446 8010

Florida's Treasure Coast
Village Group Realty
Tel: 001 561 616 9240
Web: www.villagerealtygroup.com

Continental Properties Inc
Tel: 001 561 753 0135

Re/Max Prestige Realty
Tel: 001 561 793 2869

Kentucky
Century 21
Tel: 001 859 624 5488
Web: www.jmarcumreality.com

All Star Real Estate
Tel: 001 606 780 -7827
Web: www.all-starrealestate.net

Emory Associates
Tel: 001 502 348 3006/502 460 0539
Web: www.bettyseay.com

RE/MAX Realty Unlimited
Tel: 001 859 236 8200 ext 212
Web: www.paulabboud.com

Stratton Hometown Realty & Auction LLC
Tel: 001 859 734 4943 / 859 333 1673
Web: www.shre.net

Arizona
C21 Metro Alliance
Tel: 001 623 746 51 85
Web: www.century21metoralliance.com

Realty Brokers
Tel: 001 877 970 9001 / 928 474 4651
Web: www.PaysonMountainProperties.com

Coldwell Banker
Tel: 001 1800945 1082
Web: www.movetopayson.com

C21 Metro Alliance Sedona
Tel: 001 1800 513 2121 / 928 284 04422
Web: www.landofawes.com

Los Angeles
Malibu Partners
Tel: 001 310 457 877 or +1 310 990 9330
Web: www.partnersusa.com

Paramount Rodeo Realty
Tel: 001 818 999 2030

Paramount Properties
Tel: 001 818 349 9997
Web: www.paramountproperties.com

First Team Real Estate
Tel: 001 714 9966070 / 714 342 4312
Web: www.firstteam.com/maryandterri

RE/MAX Centre
Tel: 001 818 346 7362 x 231
Web: www.remaxotb.com

Mississippi
Hyneman Homes
Tel: 001 228 806 2975
Web: www.hynemancompanies.com

Cheryl High Realty
Tel: 001 228 868 8272
Web: www.tarahigh.com

Prudential Gardner
Tel: 001 228 467 1602
Web: www.prudentialgardner.com

Coast and County
Tel: 001 228 467 9111
Web: www.baysaintlouis.com

Latter and Blum
Tel: 001 228 467 4111
Web: www.latter-blum.com

Tennessee
Coldwell Banker and Jim Henry Associates
Tel: 001 865 376 2121
Web: www.coldwellbanker.com

Angela Dawn Realty
Tel: 001 423 855 2800
Web: www.angeladawnrealty.com

Bender Realty
Tel: 001 423 472 2173
Web: www.bender-realty.com

Athens Realty
Tel: 001 423 745 6161
Web: www.athensrealty.info

Texas
Coldwell Banker
Tel: 001 361 9933117 / 361 510 4880
Web: www.coldwellbanker.com

Dirks-Park Properties
Tel: 001 361 319 6858
Web: www.parkb.com

Rabe Real Estate
Tel: 001 361 358 1255
Web: www.fnbnet.net/rabe

Rockport Properties
Tel: 001 361 729 7474 / 361 441 4701
Web: www.rockport properties.com

Key Allegro
Tel: 001 361 729 2333
Web: www.keyallegro.com

RE/MAX Metro Properties
Tel: 001 877 840 3185 / 361 994 9393
Web: www.victoriaprince.com

Virginia
Premier Properties
Tel: 001 757 930 2027 / 727 291 8844
Web: www.carmenquinnhashomes.com

Lewin & Carr Inc
Tel: 001 757 787 0901
Web: www.lewincarr.com

Ralph Dodd & Associates
Tel: 001 757 678 5377
Web: www.ralphwdodd.com

More Warfreld Glick Inc Realtors
Tel: 001 757 336 6484 / 1800 2585843
Web: www.mwgbeach.com

South Africa
Cape Town
Pam Golding Properties
Tel: 0027 218 512 633
Web: www.pamgolding.co.za

Cape Waterfront Estates
Tel: 0027 217 907 644
Web: www.capewaterfrontestates.co.za

RE/MAX Living
Tel: 0027 825 694 644
Web: www.remax-address.co.za

Hibiscus Coast
Max Prop
Tel: 0027 399 781 311
Web: www.scottburghproperty.co.za

AIDA
Tel: 0027 393 121 516 / 443 826 934
Web: www.aida.co.za

Denton Miller Real Estate
Tel: 0027 333 307 304
Web: www.natal-country-estates.co.za

Pam Golding Properties
Tel: 0027 039 682 1876
Web: www.pamgolding.co.za

Garden Route
Choice
Tel: 0027 443 431 727
Web: www.choicenet.co.za/sedge/sedgechoice.htm

AIDA
Tel: 0027 443 826 934
Web: www.aida.co.za

RE/MAX
Tel: 0027 443 825 722
Web: http://remax.gardenroute.co.za

Caribbean
CaribbeanWay
Tel: 00 514-393-3003
Email: sales@caribbeanway.com
Web: www.caribbeanway.com

Dominica
Safe Haven
Tel: 001 767 448 3394
Web: www.safehavenoffshore.com

Home from Home
Tel: 001 767 449 8593
Web: www.islandguests.com

Happy Home Realtors
Tel: 001 767 449 2789

Antigua
Tradewind Realty Limited
Tel: 1-268-462-7702
Fax 1-268-460-1081
Web: www.tradewindrealty.com

Jolly Harbour Villas
Tel: 001 268 462 3085
Web: www.jollyharbourantigua.com

ABI Realty
Tel: 001 268 460 9707

Antigua Property Investments
Tel: 001 268 460 9011
Web: www.antigua-properties.com

Puerto Rico
Triny Realty
Tel: 001 787 833 7054

Yordan Realty
Tel: 001 787 833 1700
Web: www.yordanrealty.com

Sun Coast Realty
Tel: 001 787 851 6364
Web: www.suncoastpr.com

Yauco Realty
Tel: 001 787 856 3325
Web: www.yaucorealty.com

Martinique
Lesage Immobilier
Tel: 00596 596 732 970
Web: www.lesageimmo.com

Cabinet Plisson
Tel: 00596 596 611 848
Web: www.immoplisson.com

Aurore Immobilier
Tel: 00596 596 611 848
Web: www.martinique-immobilier.com

Guadeloupe
Immovital
Tel: 00590 590 881 010
Web: www.immovital.com

AGIT
Tel: 00590 590 901 616

Promo Invest
Tel: 00590 590 325 117
Web: www.promoinvest.com

St Croix
Farchette & Hanley
Tel: 001 340 773 4665
Web: www.buystcroix.com

Hamilton Real Estate
Tel: 340 773 3300 / 800 235 9050
Web: www.PatriceKelly.biz

Coldwell Banker
Tel: 340-773-7000
Web: www.ColdwellBankerVI.com